Western Europe
in the
Middle Ages

Western Europe in the Middle Ages

A SHORT HISTORY
Second Edition

JOSEPH R. STRAYER

PRINCETON UNIVERSITY

GOODYEAR PUBLISHING COMPANY, INC.
Pacific Palisades, California

CONTENTS

PREFACE

SOME KNOWLEDGE of the history of Western Europe in the Middle Ages is necessary to understand our own civilization and the problems which it faces. Unfortunately, most people—even most students of history—never have the time to study the Middle Ages in detail. This book is an attempt to give, in the briefest space possible, an interpretation of the rise and fall, the nature and contributions, of medieval civilization.

No two scholars would agree on the contents of such an essay, and much has been omitted which would seem essential to other historians. The material which has been selected is meant to illustrate two topics which I believe are basic in the study of any civilization. First, civilization is organization and specialization. The ability of people to co-operate and the way in which they co-operate, the division of labor and the means by which this division is arranged, determine the primary characteristics of a civilization. Second, large-scale and long-continued co-operation is possible only if a people possess a common set of ideals and beliefs. For these reasons I have devoted most of my space to a discussion of medieval institutions and medieval religion. Art and literature, theology and philosophy have been mentioned only in passing, as examples of the vigor of medieval civilization, and in the hope that the reader might become sufficiently interested to look up special studies of these subjects. My own deficiencies make it impossible for me to understand much about music; it seemed better to omit this topic rather than to write about it at second hand.

This book was written during a very busy period, part of which was spent in government service in Washington. My thanks are due to all those who assisted in preparing the manuscript—to Miss Helen Durling, Mrs. Bettie Schrader, and Miss Mary Sue Sell who typed rough drafts of various chapters, to Mrs. Eileen Blumenthal who made the index, and to Mr. William Bowsky who helped with the bibliography. I am especially grateful to Miss Elizabeth D'Arcy who typed and retyped the whole manuscript, saw that spelling and capitalization were consistent, and made a very nearly perfect final copy out of a mass of corrections, insertions, and deletions.

In this second edition I have tried to take account of recent scholarly work on the Middle Ages. Some errors have been corrected, the bibliography has been updated, and my appraisal of the fourteenth century has been somewhat modified. My primary purpose has remained the same: to give an interpretation of the significance of medieval civilization, not an outline of medieval history.

J. R. S.

Introduction

WHAT WERE THE Middle Ages? The conventional answer is that they were the centuries between the fall of the Roman Empire and the beginnings of modern European civilization. Scholars have argued, and will argue endlessly, as to the exact dates of these two terminal points, but we do not have to wait for them to reach an agreement. Most historians would admit that the Roman Empire was well on its way to decline by the fifth century and that many of the characteristic elements of modern civilization were apparent by 1500. We do not have to be more precise than this—we can say that the Middle Ages run, roughly, from the fifth to the fifteenth century. There will be exceptions to this rule-of-thumb definition—aspects of Roman civilization survive in some parts of Europe long after 400 A.D. and elements of modern civilization appear in Italy well before 1500—but no student of medieval history can say that these transitional forms are completely outside his field of interest.

The Middle Ages extend from the fifth to the fifteenth century. This is a long period, so long that many writers will argue that it has no real unity, that there are many middle ages instead of one. There is force in this argument. We have only to think what our ancestors were like a thousand or even five hundred years ago to wonder whether one of Clovis's German warriors had much in common with a crusader of the twelfth century or an English baron of the Wars of the Roses. Is there any real unity in the Middle Ages, or have we simply developed a convenient catch-basket phrase in which to dump a number of centuries that do not greatly interest us?

To answer this question let us pick a century which everyone will admit was medieval, say the twelfth. How do the ways of

3

living, the basic ideas and ideals of this century differ from those of the Roman Empire and those of the modern world?

In the first place, it is clear that we are dealing with a civilization which, in its complete form, covers only Western Europe. It has little influence on Eastern Europe and even less on Western Asia and Northern Africa. Graeco-Roman civilization had been Mediterranean, not European; it attained its fullest development in Italy, Greece, Asia Minor, Syria, and North Africa. Modern occidental civilization is oceanic, not European; it is as typical of America, Australia, and parts of Asia and Africa as it is of Western Europe. In the Roman period most of Europe was a backward, colonial region, receiving its institutions and ideas from more advanced communities to the south and east. In the modern period Europe has been first the center and then a segment of a world civilization. But in the twelfth century European civilization stood by itself, neither greatly influencing nor greatly influenced by the civilizations of other continents.

In political and constitutional developments twelfth-century Europe occupies the same middle position. The Roman Empire was not a national state; it was a union of all the peoples who shared the common Mediterranean civilization under a single powerful ruler. The modern world, though it recognizes the fact of a common civilization, is divided into sovereign national states. The twelfth century knew neither the single powerful political unit nor the modern state. Nationalism and sovereignty did not exist, and although the concept of a Commonwealth of Christendom did exist, it found effective expression only in the Church, not in any secular political organization. Every man was subject to many overlapping authorities—to the local feudal lord or self-governing town in all ordinary affairs, to the more remote overlord (king, duke, or count) in special cases, to the Church in matters which concerned the welfare of Christendom and the Christian faith. This division of authority made absolutism impossible; neither the unlimited power of the Roman emperor nor the equally unlimited power of the modern sovereign state could exist under such circumstances. On the other hand, the weakness or the absence of large political units increased the cohesiveness of smaller groups. No individual could stand alone; he had to be part of a community, and the community of a village, of a town, or of a county influenced and controlled the lives of its members to a far greater extent than it does today.

This peculiar political organization was paralleled by an equally unusual religious organization. In the Roman Empire the state had controlled religion; the pagan cults were mere agencies of the government, and even the Catholic Church had had to conform to laws and administrative regulations issued by the emperor. In the modern period the churches are usually considered voluntary private associations, completely dissociated from the state, completely dependent on their own moral authority to enforce their rules. In the twelfth century the Church was an independent public authority. It claimed complete freedom of action; no secular ruler could interfere with its officials, its courts, or its laws. But at the same time, the twelfth-century Church insisted that lay authority must support its efforts to preserve the unity of the faith and the rules of Christian morality. The Church determined the values and the goals of European society; it held that lay governments were inferior, though independent, agencies whose chief duty was to deal with the sordid details of crime and punishment. The idea of a Commonwealth of Christendom found its expression in the Church, and loyalty to the Church was stronger than loyalty to any lay organization. If a secular ruler and the head of the Church clashed, right-thinking people were supposed to support the Church—and they usually did.

It is a little more difficult to appreciate the significance of the twelfth century in economic history. At first glance it would seem that there had been little change since the Late Roman Empire. Both in the fourth and in the twelfth centuries the great majority of the population of Europe was engaged in agriculture, and most of these agricultural laborers were unfree. The great difference between the two periods is that the fourth century was a period of declining economic activity, whereas the twelfth century was a period of economic expansion. The Romans of the Late Empire would have been satisfied if they could have kept production and commerce at their old level; the men of the twelfth century were making a great effort to increase production and commerce. They were clearing forests, draining swamps, building new towns, establishing new trading stations in the East, concentrating certain industries in the towns, and even experimenting with new sources of mechanical power, such as the windmill. This rapid expansion makes the twelfth century, in some of its aspects, resemble our own boom periods. For example, emigration agents in the Rhineland told German peasants the familiar story of fertile land on the eastern frontier which could be had for a song. But the controlling ideas of the twelfth century were so different from ours that the resemblances between the two economic systems are less striking than the differences. Strong community feeling and the influence of the Church made group enterprise more important than individual effort. Settlers on the frontier grouped themselves in villages for mutual protection and assistance; they did not set up individual and isolated farmsteads. The small business men of the towns formed strong associations, not only to guard their political rights but also to limit economic competition. Even the most individualistic enterprisers of the period, the great merchants who traded across the length and breadth of Europe, found that they had to be backed up by associations of their fellow merchants to enjoy any security. At the same time the Church and the governing classes were very suspicious of profit-seeking individuals. The Church feared, quite rightly, that such men would become too interested in this world to remember the next. Kings and nobles feared that the unrestrained drive for profits would undermine the social organization which gave them power. There was general agreement that economic activity should be regulated and controlled in the interests of society and that rapid growth was less important than social stability. This is not to say that the profit motive did not influence behavior in the twelfth century, but no one at that time thought that it was or should be the mainspring of human activity. Moreover, even the richest merchants were not very rich, and only a few towns had more than 10,000 inhabitants. As a result, neither individual capitalists nor the middle class as a whole had the same importance in the twelfth century that they have had in the modern world.

In art and literature, philosophy and science, formal and informal education, the twelfth century diverged sharply from the Roman tradition. It saw the beginnings of a new type of architecture in the early Gothic churches and a new type of literature in the poems of the troubadours and jongleurs. It witnessed the revival of science, long neglected by the Romans, and the first works of scholastic philosophy. The gradual development of the Universities of Bologna and Paris laid the foundations for a new system of education, characterized by formal lecture courses, examinations, and degrees. At the same time the ideal of the cultured gentleman slowly began to take shape in the active social life of the courts of southern France. We have inherited all these traditions, but it is hardly necessary to point out that they have been greatly modified by the passage of time. The Renaissance, in reviving the classical tradition, caused a sharp break in the development of medieval forms of expression, and when these forms were revived in their turn in the nineteenth century they had to be fitted into a new intellectual and material environment. Sir Walter Scott could not write medieval ballads, however much he soaked himself in Middle English poetry, and a Gothic church built around a steel skeleton is not the same kind of church as Notre Dame de Chartres. Even where there was no sharp break with the past, as in the field of science, gradual change led to almost complete transformation of values and objectives. We can see how modern physics developed from the Aristotelian works brought back to the West in the twelfth century, but we cannot think the thoughts of a twelfth-century scholar. The intellectual and artistic tradition of the twelfth century has its roots in the past and bears much of its fruit in the future, but it is clearly an independent tradition; it is neither decadent classicism nor primitive modernism.

If we try to summarize the results attained by this brief discussion we might say that the civilization of the twelfth century had characteristics which clearly separate it from the civilizations of Rome and of the modern world. It was a Western European rather than a Mediterranean or an oceanic civilization. Political power was divided among a large number of interdependent and overlapping governments rather than concentrated in a world empire or a group of sovereign national states. The Church was independent of secular authority, but it was more than a private association with limited functions; it set the standards and defined the goals for all human activities. In economics there was neither state regulation nor *laissez-faire;* instead local custom controlled farmers, artisans, and merchants in the interest of the whole community. In Gothic art, chivalric poetry, scholastic philosophy, and the university system of education the twelfth century created forms which were neither classical nor modern. These characteristics of twelfth-century civilization were not only distinct, but also interdependent; they fused into an organic whole. The economic institutions could not have existed without the political and religious institutions; the art and literature were profoundly affected by the religious and political beliefs of the age. The civilization of the twelfth century was remarkably self-sufficient and self-consistent; it had a flavor, a texture, almost a personality, of its own.

Obviously these elements of twelfth-century civilization are not duplicated exactly in any other period of the Middle Ages. But they illustrate the basic assumptions, the social habits, the aspirations of the other medieval centuries. Conscious choice and the force of external circumstances were leading Europeans toward the pattern of twelfth-century civilization long before that pattern could be fully worked out. Conscious choice and force of habit made Europeans cling to the basic pattern of twelfth-century civilization for generations, even though new activities and ideas forced modification of some of its details. There are important differences between the early and late Middle Ages, but these differences represent different stages in the development of a single civilization. From the fifth to the eighth century the wreckage of an older civilization was slowly cleared away. Western Europe gradually separated itself from the eastern Mediterranean world and worked out its own independent culture, based on Christianity, survivals of Roman institutions and ideas, and Germanic customs. The ninth, tenth, and eleventh centuries were a period of adjustment and experimentation, in which Europeans slowly and painfully discovered the most effective institutional and ideological expressions of their basic beliefs and aspirations. The twelfth and thirteenth centuries were a period of fruition, of full development of all the potentialities of medieval civilization. In the fourteenth and fifteenth centuries some aspects of medieval civilization decayed and others were slowly transformed under the impact of the new forces which the very success of medieval civilization had created. From this point of view there is real unity in the story of the Middle Ages; it is the story of the rise, development, and fall of a great civilization.

It is because the history of the Middle Ages is the history of a civilization that the subject is worth studying. The record of the rise and fall of any civilization deserves careful examination, for the basic problems of all civilizations are similar. When we fully understand how peoples of the past slowly became capable of organizing and integrating their efforts, how they accomplished their great and characteristic work, how they eventually lost their ability to do constructive work and slipped into uncreative repetition or actual regression, then we will understand more about our own civilization. The medieval experience is especially important—first, because we have more information about it than any comparable cycle—second, because it has contributed directly to our own way of life. Too many people still think that the Middle Ages are merely a stagnant pit which lies between the heights of classical and of Renaissance civilization, and that all our legacy from the past was carried over the bridges which Renaissance thinkers threw across the medieval pit to the firm ground of Graeco-Roman learning. This is true even of people who deposit money in a bank, who elect representatives to a national assembly, who rely on the precedents of the English common law, who receive degrees from universities and believe that science is an important part of education, who worship in Gothic churches, and who read books written in modern European languages. They would find their lives rather limited and unsatisfactory if they could do none of these things, and yet the basic idea of every one of these activities was worked out in the Middle Ages and not in ancient Greece or Rome. Our civilization has roots in the Middle Ages as well as in the classical period, and the medieval roots often contribute more nourishment than the classical ones. The story of medieval civilization is worth knowing, and it is that story which is told, in its barest outlines, in this book.

1

The Making
of
Europe

ROMAN RUINS

I. THE ROMAN EMPIRE

AT THE BEGINNING of the history of Europe stands the Roman Empire, and all the early part of the Middle Ages lies in the shadow cast by this great state. Yet the civilization of the Roman Empire was not wholly or even primarily European; it was based largely on the older civilizations of the Mediterranean basin. Alexander and his successors had fused Greek, Egyptian, and Syrian traditions into a common Hellenistic culture, and it was from this Hellenistic culture that the Romans drew most of their art and literature, their philosophy and religion, and even some of their ideas of government. Latin never supplanted Greek as the common language of the eastern part of the Mediterranean world, and the Romans never caught up to the peoples of the Levant in many important activities. Even at the height of the Empire, Alexandria was more important than Rome as an intellectual and artistic center, and Mediterranean trade was dominated by Syrians rather than by Italians. The great contribution of the Romans was the creation of a political organization which gave unity and peace to the Mediterranean basin for over two centuries. Peace and unity made it possible for the essential elements of the civilization of the eastern Mediterranean to be firmly established in the western part of the basin, and to spread, though less securely, beyond the Mediterranean watershed into western Spain, northern Gaul, the Rhineland, and Britain.

The Roman Empire was made by men who desired to see their state strong, and secure from any conceivable foreign danger.

The title of this chapter is borrowed from the excellent book of Christopher Dawson, which deals in detail with the matters briefly outlined in this chapter. Readers interested in the earlier part of the period will find many stimulating ideas in P. Brown, *The World of Late Antiquity*.

Rival military powers were ruthlessly destroyed, and conquered peoples were plundered that Rome might be great. During the period of rapid expansion Roman rule was always harsh and often corrupt. The only benefit it offered was the gradual extinction of international warfare, and it was difficult for suffering subjects to see that this was much of a gain. But as the position of Rome became more secure, and as Roman political institutions became more stable, the character of Roman government improved. Partly from the Greek philosophers, partly from their own experience, the Romans developed the concepts of a fundamental law binding all men, and of an ideal justice in which all should participate. Inspired by these ideals, guided by the great emperors of the second century A.D., the Roman Empire lost its predatory character and became a universal commonwealth. Inhabitants of Rome and Italy lost their special privileges, the rights of Roman citizenship were extended to almost all subjects of the Empire, and the provinces flourished in the peace and security provided by an honest and efficient government. As distinctions between conqueror and conquered disappeared, the Empire was accepted by all its subjects as a desirable and permanent form of political organization. Yet just as the Empire succeeded in creating a real community of interest and feeling in the Mediterranean basin, it began to decay. This decay is one of the great puzzles of history, and no one has ever been able to explain it in a completely satisfactory way. A partial explanation may be suggested by a discussion of certain weaknesses which existed in the Empire.

The most obvious weakness of the Roman Empire was political. The Republic had failed because it could not keep its officials from fighting for the spoils of power. Under the Empire this danger was avoided by steadily increasing the power of the emperor until no other authority in the state could resist his orders. But the imperial office was at first considered a temporary expedient and it never was placed on an absolutely permanent basis. This was especially true when it came to the question of succession. The new emperor might be the real or adopted heir of his predecessor, he might be elected by the Senate, or he might be chosen by the most powerful section of the army. No one of these methods was followed exclusively, and the uncertainty about the principle of succession frequently led to civil war. Until the third century these wars did no great damage, but after 235 there was a period of fifty years in which it seemed impossible to create a stable government. Emperors were made by intrigues in the bureaucracy or by plots in the army, and were destroyed by their rivals almost as fast as they were made. The army was occupied almost exclusively with civil wars, and barbarians raided all the provinces of the Empire and even built pirate fleets on the shores of the Mediterranean. The great generals who emerged at the end of this period of disorder, such as Aurelian and Diocletian, were finally able to restore peace and unity, but only at the price of turning the Empire into a military despotism.

This accentuated another evil which had been growing steadily since the last years of the Republic—the great majority of the inhabitants of the Empire could not participate in the work of government. The poorer classes were completely debarred from political life during the first century A.D., but the early emperors left local government in the hands of the middle class and allowed the aristocratic Senate some voice in imperial affairs. But local governments ran into financial difficulties and were not as efficient or as honest as the emperors wished, so their powers were steadily curtailed. The Senate was often a center of intrigue against the emperor, and the military despots of the third and fourth centuries would not tolerate such a rival. Senators were given great social prestige and high-sounding titles, but they were deprived of all political responsibilities. By the fourth century all significant acts of government were the work of the emperor and his companions and servants. Out of this group of men close to the emperor there gradually developed a huge bureaucracy. This imperial bureaucracy was not deliberately tyrannical, nor was it especially corrupt or extravagant. It was often harsh and inflexible, and sometimes slow and inefficient. Slowness and inefficiency drove the

Roman State another step closer to absolutism. The emperors of the period were soldiers, terribly anxious to preserve the Empire, but eager for final solutions to problems that had persisted for generations. They were apt to reduce all difficulties to military terms and to use military discipline as their only solution to all problems. When municipal officials found the burden of tax-collecting too great and tried to avoid holding office, the emperors made them hereditary servants of the state, bound to perform their unpopular duties from generation to generation. When bakers and boatmen began to find their occupations unprofitable they too were ordered to remain at their posts and to train their sons to succeed them. Small farmers who had lost their lands and had become tenants on great estates were also bound to their occupation. They could not give up their leases, nor could their landlords dispossess them; each family of tenants was to continue to cultivate the same patch of land forever. The civilian inhabitants of the Empire were to be the supply corps of the army, and like the army, they were to do their work without questioning orders or expecting special consideration for individual needs.

The lack of fixed constitutional principles had turned the Roman Empire into a military despotism. By the end of the third century the army controlled the state, and the chief problem of the emperors was to control the army. Their task was made no easier by the fact that the army was no longer a Roman army, in any sense of the word. Both political and economic pressures barred Roman citizens from military service. The emperors were suspicious of members of the upper classes who sought military distinction, and succeeded in keeping them from serving as officers. Poorer citizens, sinking into economic servitude, could not be released from their tasks for military service. By the fourth century it was no longer possible to fill the ranks of the army from the inhabitants of the Empire, and the emperors had to seek their soldiers beyond the frontiers. Thousands of barbarians, especially Germans, were taken into the army; eventually whole tribes were hired as units, fighting under the commands of their chiefs. These barbarians were brave soldiers, loyal to their generals as long as they were paid, but their discipline was not good and they were not especially devoted to the Empire. They wanted to enjoy the benefits of Roman civilization—the cleared lands, the regular food supply, the well-made clothes and fine weapons—but they did not understand the civilization which they wanted to enjoy. They could not preserve it; they could not repair and restore it when it decayed. And yet these barbarian soldiers, with their limited outlook and small sense of civic responsibility, were the source of political power in the Empire. They were the only group who could express their discontent with the government, the only group whose wishes had to be heeded by the men in power. Unfortunately for the Empire, the desires of the barbarians were always concerned with their own welfare and never with the welfare of the state. They would revolt to make a favorite general emperor, to gain extra pay, to force an allotment of land to veteran troops, to gain high offices for their native leaders. They would never revolt to change the political system which was strangling patriotism, civic responsibility, and private initiative. Like the civilians, the soldiers accepted the Empire as a natural phenomenon which was as permanent and unchangeable as the solar system. The Empire was there; they made the best terms with it they could, but it was not their job to keep it going. All responsibility, all initiative, lay with the emperor and his bureaucrats. If they failed to do their duty, if they made disastrous mistakes, no body of citizens or of soldiers could take their place or repair their errors.

The political situation was bad; the economic situation was even worse. Most of the city governments, many members of the middle class, and the great majority of peasants were bankrupt long before the fall of Rome. This impoverishment of the Empire increased the sense of strain and futility which contributed to the final collapse. Men who could not make a decent living after honest effort, men who saw their standard of living and their social status steadily diminishing, could not be expected to be very much interested in preserving a civilization which had ruined them. And yet the Empire included the richest regions and the most fertile lands of the ancient world. If Greece could prosper when it had been divided into dozens of petty states, if pre-Roman Spain and Gaul had been able to attract traders when all land and sea routes were dangerous, why should the union of these lands with many others produce a depression instead of a boom?

In the first place, the political institutions of the Empire were more highly developed than its economic institutions. Politically, the Mediterranean basin had been united in a highly centralized state; economically, it was still divided into a number of almost self-sufficient regions, many of which were economically under-developed. The Empire had to support a large bureaucracy and an even larger army; it had to defend the almost impossibly long frontiers which enclosed the Mediterranean world. The cost of the imperial government was not great by our standards, but it seemed very high to men of the fourth century A.D. The total population of the Empire was much less than that of the same regions today, which meant that each individual had to carry a larger share of the burdens of government.

Even worse, the chief occupation of the inhabitants of the Empire was agriculture, so that wealth per capita was very low. The Romans despised commerce, which remained largely in the hands of Syrians and other peoples of the Levant. This gave the eastern half of the Empire certain advantages over the West, but even in the East commerce added less to the wealth of the Empire than might have been expected. Trade in oriental luxury goods formed a large part of the stream of Roman commerce and Rome had little to offer India, Persia, and China in return for imports of silks, spices, perfumes, and precious stones. A steady stream of gold and silver flowed from the Empire to the Orient, leaving the Mediterranean world short of specie. The absence of any well-developed credit system made it impossible to replace the precious metals with paper, and the resulting disorganization of the currency made it difficult to do business of any kind. Active internal trade would have eased these monetary problems, but internal trade seems to have declined in the last centuries of the Empire. All the Mediterranean lands produced the same agricultural staples—wheat, olive oil, and wine—so that only the largest cities had to import food from any distance. There were not enough of these cities to support a flourishing grain trade, and in any case Rome and Constantinople drew their food supplies largely from the imperial estates of North Africa and Egypt. Trade in manufactured articles could not take the place of trade in food because the Romans, with abundant slave labor, never took much interest in efficient production. They used few machines; they clung to cumbersome methods of production, and in these circumstances no one manufacturing center could have any great advantages over other districts. Except for luxury articles, each province of the Empire was relatively self-sufficient, and even within the provinces rural districts drew little from the towns. Any great estate produced most of the food needed by its inhabitants, and the artisans who lived there could make all the furniture, pottery, tools, and clothing which were required. In short, the Empire was never really an economic unit, and the lack of common economic interests made disintegration easier.

Political autocracy and economic stagnation weakened loyalty to the emperor and to the Empire. The rulers of imperial Rome had tried hard enough to build up loyalty with their temples devoted to the imperial cult, their monuments and public buildings, their ceremonies and festivals. Their efforts failed—partly because the cult of emperor-worship and Rome-worship was synthetic, foisted on the people from above instead of springing spontaneously from popular beliefs and experiences—even more because the average inhabitant of the Roman Empire could take no interest in the affairs of an organization in which he played no significant rôle. At the very end of the Empire the emperors tried to use religious belief to take the place of the civic loyalty which was missing. They accepted Christianity as the religion of the state and hoped that devotion to the new religion would inspire devotion to the protectors and upholders of the faith. This attempt also failed, except in the East. In the West, Christian leaders were unwilling to bind themselves too closely to the political fortunes of the state in which they lived. They accepted the Empire as a fact; they did not insist upon it as a necessity. The greatest Christian writer of the West, St. Augustine, said that the all-important community was the Heavenly City of God, and that compared to the Heavenly City the fortunes of earthly states were unimportant. He and his friends withdrew from the service of the state, and though they performed notable works of charity and piety in their communities the Empire was nevertheless deprived of men who might have been outstanding political leaders. Moreover, the Church in the western provinces of the Empire had little influence in rural areas, where the majority of the population lived. Thus, in the West, religious conviction did not reinforce patriotism, and men who would have died rather than renounce Christianity accepted the rule of conquering barbarian kings without protest.

This leads us to the heart of the problem. The most obvious symptom of decay was the occupation of the western part of the Empire by migrating Germanic peoples. Yet there were millions of Roman citizens, compared to a few hundred thousand Germanic invaders. At any stage in the collapse of the Empire the Roman or Romanized population could have driven out the Germans and restored the unity of the state—if they had really wanted to do so. It would have cost them some lives; it would have devastated some property, but the price would not have been excessive by the standards of the early Empire. Yet the Roman population never made a move against the intruders. The bulk of the opposition was furnished by mercenaries—usually Germans themselves—who would fight only as long as they were well paid, and by a minority of Roman aristocrats who had preserved some memory of the old Roman patriotism. We can say with absolute truth that the Roman

Empire fell because the great majority of its inhabitants made no effort to preserve it. They were not actively hostile to the Empire; they were merely indifferent. The reasons for this indifference may or may not be the ones suggested above, but the fact of indifference cannot be denied. Rome had developed a well-arranged administrative system and an excellent set of laws; she had spread a common language and a common culture throughout the Western World; but she had not succeeded in making her subjects feel that they should strive actively to preserve this social and political system. This is the great failure of Rome, and it is in the shadow of that failure that the Middle Ages begin.

II. THE CHURCH

As the Roman Empire in the West slowly collapsed, the Christian Church emerged as the one stable institution among the ruins. The ablest inhabitants of the Empire became servants of the Church rather than the state, and they brought with them the Roman genius for administration and law. The men who were still capable of devotion to an ideal gave their loyalty to their faith rather than to their government. As a result, the Church had excellent leadership and strong popular support at a time when the state was weak in both respects.

The strength of the early Church lay in its uncompromising dogmatism, its ability to give certain and reassuring answers to a bewildered and discouraged people. The Empire, as St. Augustine admitted, was the most virtuous state which had ever existed; it represented the best which men inspired by purely secular ideals could achieve. Yet even at its best it fell far short of satisfying the aspirations of its subjects. It offered for the future only a repetition of the present—a rather dull prospect even if the present had been more attractive than it actually was. It was supposedly based on peace and justice, yet it could not prevent recurring civil war and harsh treatment of the poor. Worst of all, the Empire was unable to give any significance to the life of the ordinary individual. He played no part in politics; he had little economic opportunity; his only function was to produce wealth for the state and the ruling classes. The Church could promise a future life in which justice and peace would be realized; it could stress the overwhelming importance of the individual soul in the eyes of God. These were important factors in spreading Christianity among the poorer classes.

Christianity was not the only religion which appealed to the inhabitants of the Empire. Various Oriental cults, such as the religion of Mithra or the worship of Isis and Osiris, offered some of the same satisfactions. They promised immortality and the forgiveness of sin; they stressed the importance of the individual in the community of believers. They were weaker than Christianity because they were tarnished with gross superstitions and obvious inconsistencies in doctrine. They were not as sure of their exclusive possession of truth as was Christianity; they usually admitted that there was some value in the rites and beliefs of other faiths. These were fatal flaws in an age when men were anxious for positive assurance, for an ideal which could be followed without reservations. Christian doctrine was logical and self-consistent; it was expounded by men who understood and followed the basic rules of classical thought. The leaders of the Christian Church flatly refused to compromise on matters of belief, they would not dilute their faith in order to gain lukewarm adherents. As a result, Christianity spread more slowly than its rivals, but it also spread more surely. Once a Christian Church had been established it seldom went out of existence, and backsliding among individual Christians was rare. The consistency and certainty of Christian doctrine attracted men of outstanding ability, and under their leadership the new faith began to spread to the middle classes. In spite of intermittent persecution the Church grew steadily. By 300 A.D. it included a considerable minority of the population of the East and was well established in the larger towns of the West.

This was the situation when the Emperor Constantine granted first toleration and then official support to the Church. His actions cannot be explained purely on grounds of policy, since he was originally ruler of the northwestern provinces, the least Christian part of the Empire. Even if the Christians had taken an active part in politics, which they did not, Constantine had less to gain from their support than his co-emperors in Italy and the East. He seems to have become sincerely convinced of the power of the Christian God and the truth of the Christian faith. His unbroken record of victories over rival emperors strengthened his belief, and though his understanding of Christian doctrine and Christian ethics was always rudimentary, he gave unwavering support to the leaders of the Church. His successors, with one brief exception, continued his policy, and by 400 Christianity was firmly established as the official religion of the Empire.

The acceptance of Christianity by the emperors did not mean that the Church at once became the dominant influence in the lives of their subjects. The conversion of a people is not something that can be rushed through by a few edicts, and all through the early Middle Ages there was a considerable time lag between the official acceptance of Christianity by a ruler and its actual acceptance by the mass of the population. One of the great tasks of the Church after 300 was to make real Christians out of nominal Christians—an undertaking which required generations of patient endeavor. Both the organization and the doctrine of the Church had to be perfected before it could reach the position of unquestioned supremacy which it held in later centuries.

There were two main weaknesses in the organization of the early Church—inadequate provision for inhabitants of rural districts and lack of a centralized administrative system. Both weaknesses go back to the first centuries of the Church when the new faith spread from city to city, jumping over the great stretches of agricultural country which lay between the towns. The early churches were city churches; peasants could learn the new doctrine and follow its rites only if they visited the towns. They were naturally slow to become converts, especially in the West, where towns were small and scattered. As a result the *pagani*—the country dwellers—became the pagans—the typical non-Christians of the Late Empire. The complete conversion of this group did not take place until long after the fall of the Western Empire, when rural churches were built and the parish system was established. Meanwhile the city churches, which carried the entire burden of preserving and teaching the faith, had no administrative connection with each other. Each city had its own bishop, who was subject to no higher authority. It is true that the bishops of smaller towns naturally looked up to the bishops of the larger cities, and that churches founded by the apostles, such as Rome and Antioch, claimed special authority in interpreting the faith, but this hierarchy in prestige was far from being a hierarchy in administration. As long as each bishop was more or less autonomous the Church could not enforce a common policy throughout the Christian world.

The same administrative weaknesses were also evident in the monasteries, the communities of men and women specially devoted to the Christian life. Monks withdrew from the world because they felt that in an evil world they could not practice Christian virtues or devote enough time to contemplation and worship. But discipline was lax in the early monasteries. The monks did not obey their nominal head, the abbot, and, especially in the East, they became deeply involved in quarrels over doctrine. Only after a long series of reforms, culminating in the Rule of St. Benedict (soon after 500), did the western monks become a disciplined force, obedient to the orders of the Roman Pontiff.

The dangers inherent in this lack of administrative unity were emphasized by the doctrinal disputes of the fourth and fifth centuries. There had been heresies even while the Christians were a persecuted minority, but the need for standing together against a common foe had kept most of the faithful united on a common body of doctrine. The conversion of Constantine removed this reason for conformity and the spread of Christianity to the educated classes introduced all the subtleties of Greek philosophical thought. Jealousies among the different racial and linguistic groups in the East added a new element of confusion; if the Greeks of Constantinople held to one interpretation, the Egyptians of Alexandria were automatically suspicious of it. The first disputes were over the relationship of the Persons of the Trinity—was the Son coeval with the Father or was He created later? Was He in some way inferior to or subordinated to the Father? When these questions had been officially settled new arguments arose over the nature of Christ. It was generally agreed that He partook of both divine and human nature—but was the divine so dominant that it made the human unimportant, or were the two coexistent, or was the divine almost suspended when the Son took on human form? The bitter quarrels over these questions split the Christians of the East into irreconcilable groups and paved the way for the eventual loss of Syria and Egypt to Christianity. They also led to constant interference by the emperors in the affairs of the Church. The rulers of the Empire were naturally worried by religious disputes which became so violent that they led to rioting in the streets of their chief cities and to dissension among the people of their provinces. Since the Church did not possess the administrative machinery necessary to impose agreement, the emperors tried to secure uniformity through the power of the state. Constantine found it necessary to call a Church Council at Nicaea as early as 325, and his successors followed this precedent throughout the fourth and fifth centuries. In theory the bishops were to control the Councils and decide disputed questions of doctrine after free debate, but in practice the emperors had considerable influence over the conclusions which were reached. Moreover, in the intervals between Councils the emperors were able to influence the evolution of doctrine by backing bishops of one party and by exiling their opponents.

The quarrels over dogma were especially acute in the East and imperial interference in Church affairs was therefore greater in this region. As a result, the Eastern churches became accustomed to a certain degree of state control, which has persisted, in one form or another, down to our own times. Yet in spite of this constant intervention, the emperors failed to secure doctrinal unity in the East. If they tried to avoid trouble by imposing broad formulae which could be interpreted in opposite ways, they irritated all the contestants, whereas if they supported clear-cut decisions on dogma they ran the risk of alienating half or two-thirds of their subjects. By the sixth century, the great majority of the people of Egypt had flatly rejected the creed favored by the emperors and a large part of the population of Syria was also following unorthodox leaders. The Balkans and Asia Minor were the only Eastern regions which gave strong support to the orthodox faith.

The situation in the West was rather different. This region was less troubled by sectional and municipal jealousies than the East. Provincial loyalties seldom assumed the form of religious nationalism, and Rome had no rival as a Christian center in its half of the Empire. The inhabitants of the West were less interested in subtle doctrinal problems than those of the East; heretical leaders were rare and attracted few followers. The absence of serious disputes over doctrine and the unquestioned prestige of Rome made it easy for the Western churches to unite around the bishop of Rome. His leadership in spiritual matters was recognized even during the period of persecution, and was strengthened during the controversies of the fourth and fifth centuries. The backing of the Western churches gave the bishop of Rome great influence in the Councils, and the fact that the doctrines which he supported were finally recognized as orthodox increased his prestige throughout the Christian world. Although he still had no direct administrative authority, his decisions on important problems were almost universally respected in the West, and often prevailed in the East, even over the opposition of the bishops of Constantinople. The fourth-century bishops of Rome were not yet the all-powerful popes of the twelfth century, but they had laid a firm foundation on which their successors could build. They had secured sufficient administrative and doctrinal unity in the West to ensure the survival of a universal Church in a period of political disintegration.

III. THE GERMANIC MIGRATIONS

The acceptance of Christianity by the rulers of the Empire did not repair the fatal weaknesses of the Roman state. The able men who became Christian bishops and teachers did not feel that it was their duty to occupy themselves with political and economic problems. They had the tremendous task of organizing churches throughout the towns of the Empire, of converting pagans and improving the morals of nominal converts, of combatting heresy and developing Christian theology into a logical and self-consistent system. They could ensure the survival of Christianity; they could not ensure the survival of the Empire. The latter task was left to the emperors and their subordinates. These secular leaders made heroic efforts to save the state during the fourth and fifth centuries, but they were only partially successful. They could not solve the basic problem—that of interesting the inhabitants of the Empire in the fate of their government. In the West there was mere indifference; in many parts of the East there was active hostility, based on religious and cultural differences. Only in the Balkans and Asia Minor was there much support for government and only in this area was loyalty to orthodox Christianity identified with loyalty to the state. The other provinces of the Empire were unwilling or unable to defend themselves and were ready to submit to any invader.

Potential invaders could be found everywhere on the long frontiers of the Empire, but in the fourth and fifth centuries Rome's most dangerous neighbors were the Germans of Central and Eastern Europe. They were familiar enough with conditions in the Empire to covet its material resources and to realize its political and military weakness. For centuries they had been filtering across the border into the promised land, raiding when Rome was weak, enlisting in the army when she was strong. Many Roman generals and most of their troops were German, and the nominally Roman provinces along the Rhine and Danube were full of semi-civilized German tribes which had been conquered and settled in strategic locations as frontier guards.

This natural drift of Germans into the Empire was greatly accelerated in the fourth century by the sudden irruption of the Huns into Eastern Europe. The Huns were one of those nomadic peoples of Central Asia whose periodic raids have repeatedly changed the history of the great coastal civilizations of the Eurasian landmass. Ordinarily scattered and disunited, the nomads were occasionally brought together by able leaders, and when this happened they formed an almost irresistible force. Tireless and tough, inured to extremes of heat and cold, content with meager rations, spending most of their waking hours in the saddle, hitting hard and suddenly, they could be defeated only by well-disciplined troops operating under first-rate commanders. The Germans, in spite of their bravery as individuals, could offer no effective resistance to the Huns, and the wedge of nomad invaders drove through the strongest Germanic peoples into the heart of Europe. Many of the Germans became subjects or tributaries of the Huns; those who escaped this fate milled around frantically looking for a place of safety. The most obvious refuge was behind the fortified lines of the Roman frontier, and tremendous pressure built up all along the border. From the Rhine delta to the Black Sea the Germans were on the move, and the Roman government could do nothing to stop them.

Since the Germans could not be stopped, the obvious move was to regularize the situation by admitting them as allies serving in the Roman army. This policy was followed with the Visigoths, the first group to cross the frontier. It was not entirely successful, since the Visigoths became annoyed at being treated as a subject people and repeatedly revolted, asking for more land, more pay, and higher offices for their leaders. They defeated a Roman army at Adrianople in 378; they pillaged the western Balkans and moved into Italy, where they sacked Rome in 410. Then they were persuaded to continue their migration to Spain, where they drove out another group of invaders and set up a Visigothic kingdom. In spite of these excesses, the bond between the Visigoths and the Roman government was never entirely broken. They served the Empire occasionally in wars with other Germanic peoples and one of their kings died, fighting for Rome, in a great battle against the Huns in 451.

Meanwhile, the push across the frontiers continued. The Vandals marched from central Germany, through Gaul and Spain, to North Africa. The Burgundians occupied the valley of the Rhône. A mercenary army in Italy set up a king of their own in 476, the traditional date of the fall of the Empire in the West. The emperor at Constantinople could find no remedy for this situation except to send a new group of Germans, the Ostrogoths, against the usurper. The Ostrogoths, under their great leader Theodoric, were successful, but the Empire gained little, for Theodoric promptly created a kingdom for himself in Italy. Last of all, the Franks began to occupy Gaul, while the Angles and Saxons started the slow conquest of Britain.

The occupation of the Western provinces by the Germans caused less material damage than might have been expected. Almost everywhere the imperial government succeeded in keeping some sort of connection with the leaders of the occupying forces. German kings were made generals in the Roman army, given honorary titles such as consul or patrician, or even adopted into the imperial family. These were not mere face-saving devices, since they kept the Germans from treating their new possessions as conquered territory. The Romans in the West preserved their law, as much of their local government as they desired, and most of their property. The Germans had to be given land, but the West, with its thin population, had land to spare, and few of the old inhabitants had to be completely dispossessed. There was a considerable amount of pillaging and violence while the Germans were moving through the Empire, but once they had settled down they were not hostile to the Romans. There had never been any deep-rooted racial or cultural antagonism between Roman and German. Intermarriages had been and continued to be common, and the Germans had great respect for Roman civilization, as far as they understood it. They had come into the Empire to enjoy it, not to destroy it; they had not the slightest idea of wiping out the old way of life and substituting a new Germanic culture in its place.

And yet the coming of the Germans did mark the end of Roman civilization in the West. In some regions, especially along the Rhine and upper Danube, the Germans settled so thickly that the few remaining Romans could not preserve their language and customs. Britain, which had never been completely Romanized, lost practically all of its Latin civilization during the Anglo-Saxon conquest. The Romans had withdrawn their garrisons and officials before the Saxons arrived, so that there was no way to arrange for a peaceful transfer of authority. The native Britons reverted to their Celtic culture, but while this gave them enough courage to resist, it did not give them enough strength to defeat the invaders. They were forced back into the mountains, or driven to France, where they gave the name of Brittany to the Armorican peninsula. In Italy, Spain, and most of Gaul, the Germans were never numerous enough to change the fundamental characteristics of the population, but even in these regions there was a profound alteration in the organization of society and the activities of the people. Roman institutions and culture had been decaying for two centuries in the West, and the Germans were not able to put new life into a senile civilization. They were intelligent enough as individuals, but they lacked the traditions, the institutions, and the training which was necessary to understand and reinvigorate the relatively complicated system over which they had gained control.

Perhaps the greatest weakness of the Germans was in politics. The basic unit of German society was the "folk"—a group related by ties of blood and custom. Membership in the "folk" could be acquired, in most cases, only by birth, and it left an indelible mark on the one who possessed it. Wherever he went, whatever he did, he remained subject to the laws and customs of his people, or rather, he retained these laws and customs as an inalienable birthright.

Leadership of the "folk" was usually based on heredity; kings and subordinate leaders were selected from families which claimed descent from the gods. The duties of the rulers were not very heavy, since there was little government among the Germans. Most social activities were regulated by immemorial custom; personal direction by a man of high rank was necessary in only a few cases. The leaders commanded the army of free men in time of war, and even in peace were surrounded by a bodyguard of selected warriors. The leaders also presided over the assemblies of men of military age, which discussed war and peace and judged such disputes as came before them. This last duty did not take much time, since most arguments led to family feuds rather than to lawsuits. If an injured party did take his case to the assembly there was no attempt to get at the facts. Each man asserted his claim and the court invoked supernatural aid in order to determine the issue. Usually a test was set for the defendant; he must find other lawworthy men who would swear that his oath was "clean"; he must carry a hot iron several paces without serious injury; he must sink several feet when thrown into a river or lake. If the defendant met the test he went free; if he failed he paid a fine, determined by the gravity of the offense. Most Germanic law consisted in long tables of fines; it cost more to cut off the index finger than the little finger, more for knocking out a grinder than an eyetooth, more for killing a pregnant woman than one who was past the child-bearing age. The basic idea in all this procedure was to prevent a feud rather than to do justice. One side was placated by receiving money, the other by knowing that the gods had judged against it.

The German political system was directly opposed to that of the Romans in many important aspects. It was based on blood-ties and personal allegiance to a ruler rather than on loyalty to an impersonal state. It had no territorial basis; a man was a Visigoth because he was born of Visigothic parents, not because he was born within certain fixed boundaries. It was directed by unwritten custom and tradition rather than by man-made laws and administrative decisions. It demanded more of free men, in expecting all of military age to serve in the army—less, in not requiring taxes and obedience to economic regulations.

It is evident that rulers brought up in the German political tradition would find it difficult to maintain a government of the Roman type. They could not easily understand Roman political ideas and methods, and their German warriors were indignant over any attempt to change the customs of the folk. Three things especially were hard for a German king to do. He could not delegate authority with any safety, since there was no tradition of bureaucracy among his people. Political power was personal property for the Germans and a deputy always tended to become an independent hereditary ruler. This made it almost impossible to preserve the administrative hierarchy of Roman times. In the second place, the absence of a well-trained, obedient bureaucracy and the emphasis on custom made it difficult for the king to secure obedience to his orders. There were no trustworthy agents to see that they were enforced, and the political tradition of the Germans was opposed to royal interference in matters of local concern. Last and worst of all, the king could not raise money to support his government. Taxation seemed iniquitous and unnecessary to the Germans. The unpaid service of free men supplied the king with his army and courts, and they could not see the need for any other services. A king who taxed was always suspected, often with reason, of trying to increase his personal fortune.

The Germans lacked the political experience and traditions necessary to build strong states on the ruins of the Roman Empire. They were equally unable to solve the economic problems of the ancient world. Even more than in the Empire, every small district was self-sufficient; each German village normally supplied itself with the essentials of life. The Germans had imported luxuries from their neighbors and from the Mediterranean civilization, but there had never been active trade in common necessities. When they entered the Empire they could not alter the prevailing pattern of economic activity. They took over Roman estates and continued the Roman luxury trade with the East, but they certainly did not increase production or trade. Western Europe continued to be an almost purely agricultural area with few economic ties among its regions.

The same decline may be observed in intellectual and literary activities. The Roman tradition had lost most of its vitality, and the German tradition was not sufficiently developed to be used as a substitute. The Romans of the Late Empire were content with what had been done before. They imitated Virgil and Suetonius; they wrote commentaries on classical works of literature; they prepared encyclopedias which contained all essential knowledge in a few hundred pages. The Germans had their legendary stories and poems, but they could not believe that these barbaric productions were equal in value to the highly polished, sophisticated Roman works. The German stories survived as part of the oral tradition of the northern peoples, but it was centuries before any of them were written down. Meanwhile, there was great respect for the Roman intellectual and literary tradition, but little understanding of it. Few of the Germans ever mastered the art of reading Latin, and the great majority of the Romans cared as little for the survival of their literature as they did for the survival of the imperial government. The Church, which depended on the written word—the Latin Bible and the writings of the Fathers—had to make some effort to preserve learning, but even churchmen were often satisfied with elementary treatises on grammar, and little compilations of extracts from the classics. There were a few truly learned clerics and most bishops and abbots could read and write Latin after a fashion, but even among the clergy the level of education was low. The level outside the Church was even lower; by 800 an educated layman was rarely found outside Italy.

The disappearance of educated laymen contributed to the political and economic weakness of the Germanic kingdoms. With no literary standard to preserve linguistic unity, colloquial Latin split into dozens of different dialects. The absence of linguistic unity made it hard to secure political unity. For example, the people of Aquitaine, who did not speak the same dialect as the people of the Seine valley, were suspicious of rulers who came from the north. The fact that most laymen could not read or write made it difficult to carry on the normal functions of government. The central authorities received few written reports from local governors and they could never be sure that their orders were either understood or enforced. In the end, the only way to overcome this difficulty was to use the one educated group, the clergy, as agents of government. This merely shifted the focus of the problem, since the clergy claimed independence of lay authority. The decline in the general level of education also affected the study of law; the highly developed and essentially equitable Roman legal system could not be preserved by illiterate statesmen. Roman law survived in Spain, southern Gaul, and Italy only as a set of customs little less crude than those of the Germans. In northern Gaul, the Rhineland, and Britain it was completely forgotten. Finally, the majority of the scientific and technical treatises of the ancient world were lost, either temporarily or permanently, during the period of the migrations. A few Roman works on agriculture, architecture, engineering, and the art of war were preserved, but were not studied with any care during the first centuries of the Middle Ages. Scientific works written in Greek had even less influence. The Romans, an over-practical people, had never been greatly interested in scientific theory and had never taken the trouble to translate the books which contained the great scientific discoveries of the Greeks. In the last century of the Empire few men educated in the West studied Greek, and the Greek scientific tradition had been almost forgotten before the final collapse of Roman rule in the West. Boethius, the last of the old Roman scholars, realized the danger, and in the early sixth century outlined an ambitious plan for Latin translations of the more important Greek works. But one man could do little, and Boethius' labors were first slowed down by his interest in politics, and then abruptly terminated by his execution on charges of treason to the Ostrogothic king of Italy. His work was not continued, and Western Europe possessed only fragments of the Greek scientific tradition until the great twelfth-century revival of learning.

IV. THE END OF MEDITERRANEAN UNITY

The slow decay of the Roman Empire did not at first affect the unity of Mediterranean civilization. There had been growing dissatisfaction with that civilization, but it had endured so long that it was not easy to conceive of an alternative way of life. The Germanic kingdoms of the West clung to the old forms as well as they could; they were not very civilized, but what scraps of civilization they possessed were Roman. The East was still united under the emperor at Constantinople, who governed through the old Roman bureaucracy under the forms of Roman law. Relations between East and West, while not intimate, were on the whole amicable. With the exception of the Anglo-Saxon rulers of Britain, the Germanic kings recognized the nominal suzerainty of the emperor, and he maintained the fiction of a united empire by conferring honorary titles on the barbarian monarchs. The pope was in close contact with the patriarchs of the East and maintained a representative in Constantinople. Syrian traders carried oriental goods into the heart of Gaul and even settled in small groups in the Loire River towns. Western Europe was more provincial than it had been in the great days of Rome, but it was still part of the Mediterranean world, not the seat of an independent civilization.

Yet within the Mediterranean unity, separatist tendencies were developing, and these tendencies were strongest in the East. The Germans had lowered the level of Roman civilization, but they had no rival civilization to set in its place. In the East there were rival civilizations, long suppressed but strangely potent. The Greeks and the Romans had ruled Syria and Egypt for over seven hundred years, and yet Graeco-Roman civilization had not stifled the old native cultures. It had formed a thin hard crust on top of a fermenting mass of old beliefs and institutions, and as the crust cracked under the strains of the third and fourth centuries the obscure folk-ways of the native populations began to bubble out into sight. Every student of the Late Roman Empire has noticed the revival of oriental forms and beliefs—in government, in religion, in art and literature. At first it was possible to absorb these oriental ideas into the dominant Graeco-Roman culture. The emperors assumed some of the trappings and many of the powers of an oriental despot; the most popular religions were modified versions of oriental faiths; the prevailing art-forms showed the influence of oriental motifs. But as the movement continued it became impossible to fit it into the old pattern of Mediterranean civilization. The Latin West would accept only a minimum of oriental influence, and from the fourth century on, it also became more and more suspicious of Greek ideas. The thoroughly Greek quarter of the Empire, centered around Constantinople, could not entirely abandon its odd intellectual traditions, and still sought to impose them on the rest of the East. Egypt and Syria, where the oriental revival was strongest, either had to compromise or drop out of the orbit of Graeco-Roman civilization.

If this was a dilemma for the peoples of the Roman Orient, it was also one for the emperors at Constantinople. They had not given up their claim to rule the whole Mediterranean world, and they had not abandoned hope of making their claim good. But if they went too far in satisfying Syria and Egypt they offended the Latin West and the Greeks of Asia Minor and the Balkans. If they rejected the ideas of Syrian and Egyptian leaders, they might conciliate the Greeks and the Latins but they would lose the loyalty of their wealthy oriental provinces. If they compromised they ran the risk of alienating both the West and the Orient while gaining only doubtful support from the Greeks. They could not consistently follow any of these policies, and their vacillations only intensified the growing antagonisms among the peoples of the Mediterranean.

Since religion was the most vital force in the Mediterranean world, the divisions among Latins, Greeks, and Orientals took the form of religious disputes. The bitterness of the arguments about the Persons of the Trinity and nature of Christ seems foolish unless we realize that it was a manifestation of profound cultural differences. Antioch and Alexandria would not accept the domination of Constantinople, and Rome, strong in its orthodoxy, was angered by any attempt to placate the Syrian or Egyptian heretics. The people of Constantinople developed their own brand of orthodoxy, which was neither that of Rome nor that of Alexandria, and rioted against any emperor who threatened to compromise it. A very strong emperor might have been able to force the peoples of the East to accept a common statement of religious beliefs if he had not had to worry about the opposition of the pope at Rome. Conversely, agreement between Rome and Constantinople could be secured only by losing the religious, which meant in the end the political, allegiance of Egypt and Syria.

These were the strains which made the reign of the great Justinian (527–565) a spectacular failure instead of a world-changing success. Justinian was the last emperor who had both the ability and the opportunity to restore the political unity of the Mediterranean world. Taking advantage of family quarrels in the Germanic kingdoms he reconquered Italy from the Ostrogoths, North Africa from the Vandals, and southeastern Spain from the Visigoths. The price was high in both human and financial terms, but not too high if there had been a real desire for unity in the Mediterranean basin. As it was, Justinian exhausted and angered the East without gaining the loyalty of the West. The East paid heavy taxes to support the wars of reconquest; Syria was devastated by Persian invasions which could not be repelled while the bulk of the army was in the West; Egypt saw its most cherished religious convictions attacked in order that the emperor might secure the support of the Roman Church. The West, for which all these sacrifices were made, found the imperial government no improvement over that of the barbarians. Taxes, which had been dwindling away, were reimposed; areas which had been unharmed by the Germans were devastated in the wars of reconquest; the imperial bureaucracy interfered with local autonomy without giving many benefits in return. Even Justinian's most successful enterprise, the modernization and codification of Roman law, was in some ways a failure. Roman law was the greatest and most characteristic achievement of the Romans; it represented the best in their political theory and practice. Justinian's version, with all its weaknesses, was worthy of the Roman legal tradition, and in happier circumstances might have become a symbol of political unity, like the English common law or the American Constitution. As it was, it stirred up no great enthusiasm anywhere in the Empire. Justinian's code had to be modified almost at once in the East in order to meet local conditions and it was not even applied in the West. It was to have incalculable influence on Western thinking six centuries later, but for the moment it was a dead letter.

Even before Justinian's death a new horde of barbarians, the Lombards, were pushing into Italy from the north. They soon overran two-thirds of the peninsula, and though the Empire retained a few fragments of Italian territory its hopes of maintaining a dominant position in the western Mediterranean basin were gone forever. Catastrophe in the East did not come quite so rapidly, but when it struck it was even more devastating. The latent hostility of the Oriental peoples to Graeco-Roman supremacy crystallized around the Arab Empire and permanently separated the southern and eastern shores of the Mediterranean from the civilizations of the north and northeast.

The Arabs, like the Germans, were a small, rather poorly organized group of peoples, who had raided the Empire intermittently for centuries without constituting a real military danger. Nothing shows the weakness of the old Mediterranean civilization in its last days quite so clearly as the fact that these weak border peoples could change the fate of millions with only a slight effort. The results are out of all proportion to the cause unless we realize that the invaders, German or Arab, merely set off a reaction which was already prepared. They were the detonators, but the explosives were already stored up in the Mediterranean basin. The Arabs had probably grown in numbers during the sixth century, and Mohammed gave them a better organization than they had ever had before, but the whole population of Arabia was less than that of many imperial provinces. Once more the Empire was to lose wide territories because there was no real interest in preserving its authority, no common loyalty to hold its people together.

Mohammed was a man of great ability and it was only through his efforts that the Arabs were able to take advantage of the opportunities on their northern frontiers. Like many of his countrymen, he was dissatisfied with the rather crude religion of Arabia, which often was no better than fetish-worship. He had heard fragments of the Christian story; he had met Arabic-speaking Jews who told him some of their traditions; he was familiar with Arabic legends which were not unlike the stories of the Hebrew prophets. Brooding over this material, he became convinced that God had chosen him as the last and greatest of the prophets, as the bearer of the final revelation to man. The new doctrine, as it finally emerged in Mohammed's sermons and conversation, had enough familiar elements in it to be acceptable to many of the peoples of the East. He taught that there was one all-powerful God, the creator of the world, the protector and judge of mankind; that God had revealed His will to men through a series of prophets, of whom the greatest were Abraham, Jesus, and Mohammed; that those who believed His prophets and obeyed His commandments would enjoy Paradise whereas the wicked were to suffer endlessly. After a discouraging start, Mohammed began to gain followers and eventually converted most of the tribes of northern and central Arabia to his new religion.* His original concept of his rôle seems to have been that of a purely religious leader, but he soon learned that he could spread his faith only by becoming head of a political organization which would protect his followers from the unenlightened, and suppress family and tribal feuds among the faithful. At his death in 632 he was ruler of a large part of the Arabian peninsula. There were still tribes which had not accepted his political and religious leadership, but they were too weak to form an effective opposition.

Mohammed had given the Arabs their first effective political organization, and his immediate successors profited more from this than they did from his promulgation of a new faith. Like all new religions, Mohammedanism was slow to sink into the minds and hearts of the people. The Arabs and their neighbors did not become fanatical Moslems overnight, and the great Arab conquests of the seventh century were the result of political, not religious, imperialism. Mohammed's successors, the Caliphs, could not claim to be prophets, and the only way in which they could maintain their position of leadership was by military success. They sent out raiding parties against the nearest imperial provinces and were amazed to find little resistance. Almost without planning it,

* Mohammed called his faith Islam (submission to the will of God). His followers were called Moslems.

they became involved in a conquest of Syria and Egypt. The native populations were not alarmed by the change of rulers; in fact, they often preferred the tolerant Arabs to the Greeks who had been accusing them of heresy. The old Persian kingdom, even weaker than the remnants of the Roman Empire, was also overrun by the Arabs, and the Caliphs soon found themselves masters of the whole Middle East. With this solid block of territory at their disposal, it was easy for them to push along the North African coast, and in 711 to cross into Spain. By 720 the Arab Empire stretched from the borders of India to the Pyrenees and Arab raiders were plunging deep into the heart of Gaul.

As a result of the Arab conquests, the last remnants of Mediterranean unity were destroyed, and three sharply contrasted civilizations arose within the old Graeco-Roman sphere of influence. The growth of Moslem sea power and naval wars between Greeks and Arabs made it difficult, though not impossible, for Christians to use the Mediterranean. Land travel between East and West had always been slow and expensive. Religious differences emphasized the physical difficulties of communication. The Arab Empire gradually became thoroughly Mohammedanized—suspicious and scornful of Christian institutions and ideas. The loss of Syria and Egypt combined with the mortal danger from the Moslems intensified the peculiar religious patriotism of the Eastern Empire. This led in turn to a series of quarrels between the popes and the patriarchs of Constantinople. After many schisms, a final break came in 1054 when the Roman Catholic and Greek Orthodox Churches solemnly excommunicated each other. The religious break was merely a symptom of the growing estrangement between East and West. The inhabitants of the Byzantine Empire* felt immeasurably superior to the barbarous peoples of the West

---

* With the loss of Egypt and Syria, the Eastern Roman Empire was dominated by the city of Constantinople, formerly known as Byzantium. As a result, the Eastern Empire is called the Byzantine Empire after the sixth century.

and dealt with them only for reasons of political and economic convenience. The Westerners viewed the East with suspicion and resentment. The political bond between the three areas had vanished completely; economic contacts were, for a time, somewhat reduced, and the cultural patterns which sometimes spread from one region to another were neither numerous nor strong enough to create a common civilization. The Arab Empire, the Byzantine remnant of the Roman Empire, and Western Europe each worked out its own system of institutions and beliefs.

In this shattering of Mediterranean unity it was Western Europe which had the most to lose. The Moslems had inherited much of the learning of the Greeks, and to this they added significant material from Persia and India. On these extensive foundations they were able to build a great structure of philosophical and scientific thought which made them leaders in these fields for centuries. They occupied the key position on the ancient trade-route between East and West and made the most of their opportunity by building up an active commerce and thriving industries. Even when, in the ninth century, the Arab Empire broke up into smaller states, Moslem civilization retained its essential unity and ideas and goods moved easily from India to Spain. At a time when the largest Western towns were mere fortified villages, when the most learned men of the West were painfully studying commentaries and encyclopedias, the Moslems had great commercial cites and scholars who were making original contributions in almost every field of science.

The Eastern Roman Empire was not quite so impressive as the Arab Empire, but it was still an important center of civilization. The wealth of Constantinople, the manpower of Asia Minor, and a sophisticated diplomatic and military tradition gave it unusual strength and resilience. With its rich heritage of Greek and Christian culture it developed a remarkable civilization—conservative but not decadent, orientalized but not oriental, profoundly Christian but not theocratic. It could no longer claim to be a universal empire, and though it kept the name of Rome in official documents, it was the Empire of the Greeks, of Constantinople, or of Byzantium to most outsiders. Its political boundaries were contracted, but its sphere of influence spread far beyond the narrow limits of the Byzantine provinces. The Slavic peoples of the Balkans usually admitted the hegemony of the emperor and took their basic concepts of religion, art, and literature from Constantinople. The Russians were converted by the Greek Orthodox Church and so the stream of Byzantine culture flowed into the great plains of Eastern Europe. Thus the division between East and West, which had begun in the last days of the old Roman Empire, was extended far beyond the limits of the Mediterranean basin.

The Byzantine Empire was not quite as foreign to the peoples of Western Europe as the Arab Empire, but this did not always make for better relations. The Moslem countries were outside the Christian world; everyone expected them to be different and strange. But the Byzantine Empire was Christian, though schismatic; it was based on the classical tradition, though modified by influences which had had little effect on the West. The peoples of the West always expected the inhabitants of the Byzantine Empire to be more like themselves than they really were, and were bitterly disappointed when they found that their assumption was wrong. Members of a single family will criticize conduct in their relatives which they find perfectly normal in strangers, and Western Europe and the Byzantine Empire were more or less in the position of cousins, each of whom thinks the other is betraying the family tradition. This difficulty did not end with the Middle Ages; even today we implicitly assume that Russia and the Balkans are bound by the western tradition, in spite of their heritage from Byzantium and their long exposure to oriental influences. As a result, we experience the same sort of deceptions which poisoned relations between East and West during the Middle Ages.

Western Europe was the weakest and poorest of the three areas which emerged from the old Mediterranean world. It had always been backward, both economically and intellectually, but in the classical period it had been able to draw on the East both for supplies and ideas. Now it had to face its own deficiencies without outside aid. The southern shores of the Mediterranean had become, and were to remain, a completely foreign region, while mutual suspicion between Westerners and Byzantines made it impossible to rely on Constantinople for leadership. The dangers of Mediterranean travel reinforced the psychological obstacles and threw the West back on its own resources.

These resources were not very great. On the material side, the West was an almost exclusively agricultural region. It contained some of the best farming land in the world, but much of this land was not yet cleared, and the part which was used was cultivated by inefficient methods. A few Italian towns, such as Venice and Amalfi, kept up trade with the East, and the Scandinavians managed to import some oriental luxuries across the plains of Russia; otherwise there was little commerce. Industry was at an even lower level; few craftsmen produced for more than a limited, local market. As a result the population was thin, poor, and scattered. The governments of the Germanic kingdoms were weak and unstable, unable to prevent disorder at home or to ward off attacks from the outside. Intellectually and spiritually the situation was almost as bad. The West had retained only part of its legacy from Rome, which at best was only part of the whole body of classical learning. Even this small fraction of the classical heritage was studied largely in the monasteries and was not yet fully understood. The Roman version of Christianity had no serious rivals in the West, but it had not yet made much of an impression on the people. They were Christian because they could be nothing else, but the Church in the West was too disorganized, and in many places too corrupt, to give them much leadership. Altogether, the situation of Western Europe in the seventh century was not promising. It had a rudimentary economic system, and an even more rudimentary political organization; it had inherited a few ideas about government and law, and a somewhat larger body of philosophical and literary material from Rome; it had accepted Christianity but had not yet developed either a well-organized Church or wide-spread individual piety. Western Europe was now on its own, but no one in the seventh century could have predicted that it would develop a civilization which would rival those of Bagdad and Byzantium.

V. THE WORK OF CHARLEMAGNE

We have been discussing Western Europe as a unit, in contrast to the Moslem and Byzantine Empires. This assumption was valid only for purposes of general comparison. The regions of Western Europe resembled each other more closely than any one of them resembled Syria or Asia Minor, but there were sharp differences between Frankish Gaul and Anglo-Saxon England, between Lombard Italy and Bavarian or Saxon Germany. The social and cultural heritage from the Roman Empire was unevenly exploited and was combined with new elements in different proportions by the people of each area. For example, the most active center of classical studies in the seventh century was in the British Isles, whereas Gaul, which had been much more thoroughly Romanized, rather neglected the work of scholarship. The authority of the pope was more respected in England, which had been converted by monks whom he had sent out from Rome, than it was in the Lombard kingdom of Italy, which was politically hostile to Rome. The line between Roman and German still existed in Italy and Gaul, and the distinctions between Frank and Lombard, Saxon and Bavarian were even greater. Each of these peoples "lived their own law," to use the expressive phrase of that period; they had their own customs, institutions, and beliefs which were not shared with their neighbors. Until some of these sharp differences were erased, Western Europe could not have even the foundation of a common civilization.

Uneven development was equally conspicuous in the political sphere. In the seventh century there was only one state in Western Europe which had any real strength, the kingdom of the Franks. The Anglo-Saxons in England were divided into small, warring principalities; the Visigothic kingdom of Spain was torn by internal feuds and was soon to be wiped out by the Moslems; the Lombards in Italy had never conquered the whole peninsula and were weakened by frequent civil wars. But the Franks held most of Gaul and much of the Rhine valley in Germany, as well as an uneasy suzerainty over Aquitaine and Bavaria. Their center of power was in the north, between the Seine and the Rhine, so that they were not greatly hurt either by the conquests of Justinian or the later expansion of the Arabs. They had acquired enough of the Roman idea of the state from their occupation of Gaul to rise somewhat above the limited Germanic concept of the "folk," but they had retained enough contact with Germany to secure first-class fighting men.

The Frankish kingdom was strong, however, only in comparison with its neighbors. It had suffered from the same weaknesses which had ruined other Germanic kingdoms. It was difficult for the ruler to maintain his authority over outlying dependencies, such as Aquitaine. High officials and great land-owners were rebellious and disobedient even in the heart of the kingdom. Frankish monarchs had treated their domains as private property and had repeatedly divided them among their sons. There was bad feeling between the Germanic districts of the east and the more Romanized western provinces. Altogether, the seventh-century Frankish kingdom did not offer a very secure foundation on which to build a new European civilization.

Yet from these unpromising materials a Frankish family was able to create an empire in which German, Roman, and Christian elements were fused to form a common way of life. This family, called Carolingian from its greatest representative, Charles the Great or Charlemagne, came originally from the borderlands between Gaul and Germany. It first appears as a group of great landholders, German in blood and outlook, only slightly influenced by Latin and Christian ideas. The earliest Carolingians were as selfish and short-sighted as most of their wealthy neighbors— they struggled for land and power, and did not hesitate to oppose the king or to precipitate civil war if it was to their advantage to do so. As they became more prominent in the affairs of the kingdom they gradually developed more sense of responsibility and more interest in religion and learning. Their rise to power was made easier by the existence of a peculiar Frankish institution— the mayorship of the palace. Originally this office may have been no more than the stewardship of the king's household, but since the mayor was in close personal contact with the king he gradually became a sort of prime minister. All the business of the central government passed through his hands, and a capable mayor often had more power than a weak king. The great men of the realm naturally sought this office, and during the seventh century it became the prize of civil war. The kings of this period were weak both physically and morally; most of them died young and accomplished little during their brief lives. The mayors of the palace controlled the government and the great landowners tried to control the mayors. The mayor was usually the leader of a faction of the oligarchy and held office until some other group gained strength enough to pull him down. In this welter of intrigue and violence the Carolingians had remarkable success. Members of the family held the mayorship repeatedly, and finally Charles Martel, the grandfather of Charlemagne, gained permanent possession of the office in 717. His son, Pippin, succeeded him as mayor, and in 751 felt strong enough to depose the nominal king and take the crown for himself. The dynasty thus established ruled Western Europe until the end of the ninth century and during its two hundred years of power established a common civilization for the peoples of the West.

What were the objectives of this remarkable family? The basic plan seems to have been to unite all the peoples of the West into a single Christian kingdom. Force had to be used to overcome immediate opposition, but the Carolingians were wise enough to realize that force alone would never give them a secure position. They had to gain the loyalty of their subjects by giving them a common set of ideals, and the only ideals which could be accepted by all the inhabitants of the West were those of Christianity. Therefore, the Carolingians consistently and energetically supported missions to the pagans (usually led by monks), and reform movements among the nominally Christian inhabitants of their empire. They used the Church for their own purposes, but they gave the Church more influence over the peoples of the West than it had ever had before. With the moral authority and the universally accepted ideals of the Church behind them, they found it possible to override many regional and racial differences and to legislate for Europe as a whole.

This policy was foreshadowed by Charles Martel, who encouraged missionary work in Frisia and central Germany. Pippin made the idea clearer by creating what was practically an alliance between his family and the Church. He requested papal approval for his assumption of the kingship and strengthened his position even more by having himself anointed king when the pope visited Gaul a few years later. He was the first Western ruler to receive this unction, and the ceremony greatly increased the prestige of his family. Pippin was now the Lord's anointed, the officially recognized lieutenant of God on earth. He had become a semi-ecclesiastical personage and rebellion against him was not only a crime, but also a sin. In return he protected the pope against the Lombards and fought successfully against them in Italy. In his own dominions he continued his father's policy of encouraging missionaries and reformers. Greatest of these was the Anglo-Saxon Boniface, who spent almost forty years in converting the eastern Germans and reorganizing the Frankish Church. The first task was easier than the second, for most of the Germans across the Rhine were either nominal Christians or lukewarm pagans and were quite willing to follow a man who spoke with authority. The real difficulty was to build a centralized system of church government which would ensure co-operation among Christians of the Frankish Empire and subordinate local bishops to the pope. Charles Martel and Pippin gave Boniface steady support in this effort, which smoothed the path for their own policy of centralization, and by the end of his life Boniface had improved the discipline of the clergy and greatly increased papal authority in both Gaul and Germany.

Charlemagne added little that was new to the basic family policy, but he continued it in such an intensive form that it began to yield striking results during his reign. He did not merely support the pope against the Lombards; he annihilated the Lombard kingdom and annexed two-thirds of Italy to the Frankish domains. He was not satisfied with the slow progress of missions among the remaining heathen east of the Rhine; he made relentless war on Saxons and western Slavs until they accepted the Christian faith and Frankish government. He used all his authority to preserve discipline among the clergy, and he tried to raise a new generation of churchmen who would accept discipline through conviction rather than through coercion. His rough and ready methods did not always bring immediate success, but Charles showed that he deserved his name of the Great by adhering steadfastly to his ends while modifying his means. When penal laws and military force failed to complete the conversion of the Saxons he substituted persuasion and intensified missionary activity. When legislative threats failed to purify the clergy he began a great campaign to improve their education and succeeded in raising both their intellectual and their moral standards. He also encouraged the development of the parish system, which had begun much earlier among the Franks, and made it a really effective agency for spreading and maintaining Christianity among the great masses of the rural population. The parish, centered around a village church, was a logical answer to the weakness of the older system which required a predominantly rural population to attend city churches. But bishops had had little authority over parish priests, and the priests, in turn, had often been dependent on casual offerings, and had not been treated with great respect by their parishioners. Charlemagne definitely subordinated the parish priests to the bishops, just as the bishops were subordinated to the newly established archbishops. At the same time, he gave the parish clergy an assured income and far greater authority over laymen by establishing a system of compulsory tithes and by encouraging the practice of hearing confessions.

In the light of this policy, carried on without faltering for forty-six years, Charlemagne's assumption of the title of emperor was a logical and necessary step. There has been endless and unprofitable discussion about the ceremony held on Christmas Day in 800, but certain conclusions seem well established. In the first place, Charlemagne received the title from the pope because he wanted it. He was absolute master of the Church; the pope depended on him for protection against dangerous enemies, and it is inconceivable that an act of such importance could have been planned without the king's consent. In the second place, the imperial title added nothing to Charlemagne's *political* authority. He was already ruler of most of Western Europe and he gained no new lands or rights by becoming emperor. Finally, the real advantage of the coronation was increased *spiritual* authority; it emphasized Charlemagne's position as head of Western Christendom. There were many kings, but there was only one emperor in the West. The old Roman tradition of imperial control over the Church had not been forgotten, and Charlemagne could claim to be heir to this authority. Convinced as he was that he could rule his empire only through an appeal to Christian ideals, his new title gave him an additional right to make such an appeal. It was an official confirmation of his position as defender of the faith, protector of the papacy, and vice-gerent of God on earth.

From another point of view, the imperial coronation was a

declaration of independence by the West. The shadowy suzerainty of the Byzantine Empire, recognized in papal documents as late as 772, was ended. Western Europe was no longer a spiritual and intellectual dependency of Constantinople; it was now self-sufficient in all things. The Byzantine court understood this clearly; it protested vigorously at the time, and was never quite reconciled to the existence of a line of Western emperors. Neither protests nor temporary compromises made any difference in the essential fact—Byzantium was now almost as foreign to Western Europe as Bagdad.

The Carolingian age saw the establishment of a Western European culture, strong enough to endure terrific strains, independent enough to keep its identity when brought into contact with other traditions, broad enough to include all the peoples of Western Europe, rich enough to develop new forms and ideas from its own resources. By reforming and strengthening the Church, the Carolingians made a nominally Christian Europe really Christian. The great mass of the population was in constant contact with Christian doctrine through the services held in the parish churches, confessions to the parish priest, and visits of bishops and other supervisory authorities. Some clergymen were still immoral, illiterate, and incompetent, but the Carolingian reforms had reduced the number of unworthy priests and prelates. Everywhere in Europe there were churchmen who were well-educated, intelligent, and pious; everywhere in Europe there were laymen who resolutely supported Christian ideals. As a result, a European conscience developed, based on Christian ethics—a conscience which could be easily aroused by spiritual leaders. There was plenty of brutality and stupidity in the centuries after Charlemagne, but it no longer passed without protest as it had in the earlier barbarian kingdoms. Reform movements succeeded each other with hardly a break from the tenth to the thirteenth century, and each wave of reform played a part in shaping medieval civilization.

In the field of education and learning the Carolingian age saw the establishment of a common basis for European scholarship. The works of the Church Fathers and Latin secular writers were copied, studied, and digested. The mere physical effort of copying older manuscripts had important consequences. Many works have survived only because they were copied in the Carolingian period; many others became better known because they were reproduced in different regions by Carolingian scribes. The Carolingian revival almost ended the loss of classical learning; very little disappeared in the post-Carolingian centuries compared to the wastage of the Late Roman Empire and the barbarian kingdoms. Even more important was the diffusion of ancient learning throughout Western Europe. Gallo-Romans, Anglo-Saxons, Franks, Scots from Ireland, and Lombards all studied and worked together at the courts of the Carolingian rulers. Great monasteries in England, France, Italy, and Germany built up collections of manuscripts and trained scholars to use them. These centers of learning were still widely separated, for not every monastery had the teachers or the resources necessary for scholarship, but there were enough of them to arouse interest in learning in every region of Europe. The work of Carolingian scholars was not especially original (with a few striking exceptions), but originality was not what was most needed at the time. The legacy from the past had to be assimilated before new steps could be taken, and Carolingian writers performed this task admirably. In their commentaries they demonstrated the necessity for consulting and correlating many different sources; in their treatises they restated what they had learned in their own words. These were particularly valuable exercises at a time when Latin was ceasing to be a spoken language, when the rise of local dialects was depriving the peoples of Europe of a common tongue. Latin was needed for serious thinking on any subject, since the new dialects had serious deficiencies in vocabulary. It was even more necessary for purposes of inter-European communication, since no other language covered more than a local area. If medieval Europe possessed a common fund of ideas, it was largely due to the work of Carolingian scholars.

Carolingian government was not entirely uniform—each major part of the empire kept its own laws and customs—but it did tend to lessen the sharp distinctions which had prevailed between different peoples. The old division between Roman and German practically disappeared during the Carolingian period and the basis of law tended to be territorial rather than personal. For example, the people of Burgundy now settled their disputes by referring to a single set of customs; they were no longer divided into groups "living" Burgundian, Frankish, or Roman law. Moreover, there were institutions and laws which were common to the whole empire. The county administered by a count was the basic unit of local government, and the counties long survived the collapse of the Carolingian monarchy. Coinage and weights and measures also followed the Carolingian pattern for centuries in most European countries. Newly acquired territories such as Italy and Saxony were usually governed by men who came from the older Frankish domains, and this also tended to establish a degree of uniformity. As a result, there came to be a certain similarity in the laws and institutions of most Western countries, and it was not difficult for men of one region to fit into the political systems of other areas.

At the end of the Carolingian period Europe, for the first time, formed a distinct political and cultural unit. It had separated from the worlds of Byzantium and Islam; it had its own traditions and characteristic patterns of behavior. In spite of local differences a European felt at home in any European region, but he was immediately conscious of being in a foreign country when he visited Constantinople or Cordova. This establishment of a specifically European tradition was the great and enduring work of the Carolingian family. The empire fell; the facts of Carolingian history were forgotten, but the impression remained that the reign of Charlemagne marked a turning-point in the development of

Western Europe. The wildest legends about the great emperor still contained the essential truth—the belief that he stood at the beginning of Western European civilization. The strange and wonderful structure of European civilization still rests on the foundations laid in the age of Charlemagne.

2

The Years of Transition

CHARLEMAGNE'S CHURCH AT AACHEN
A reconstruction

I. THE COLLAPSE OF THE CAROLINGIAN EMPIRE— FEUDALISM

THE CAROLINGIAN EMPIRE was a political miracle, and like all miracles it could be but a temporary interruption in the natural course of events. Christianity had given Western Europe common ideals, but the ties of material interests, which are also necessary to bind men together, were lacking. There was little trade between different parts of the Empire; each region was largely self-sufficient. Communications were slow and difficult; even an intelligent and energetic ruler like Charlemagne found it hard to secure information or to enforce his orders. Local government was the only government which concerned most inhabitants of the Empire, and local government was in the hands of the counts, wealthy and powerful men who were very independent of central authority. It is not surprising that the Carolingian Empire began to break up within a generation of the great emperor's death; it is surprising that it had held together long enough to produce permanent results.

The strong tendency toward political and economic localism was the basic weakness of the Empire; other factors only hastened its decline. The successors of Charlemagne did not inherit his ability; the traditional epithets attached to their names emphasize defects, not abilities. Louis the Pious, Louis the Stammerer, Louis the Child, Charles the Bald, Charles the Fat, Charles the Simple— these are not the names of powerful and respected rulers. Most of the later Carolingians strove earnestly to preserve the Empire and its institutions; none of them possessed the incredible energy, the political insight, the art of commanding men which had made Charles great.

The rule of primogeniture was not yet established in Europe; the Empire, like any other inheritance, was divided among the sons of the Carolingian house. Charlemagne himself had planned to share his lands among his children, but premature deaths left him oniy one heir. Charles's only surviving son, Louis the Pious, spent the last half of his life trying to work out a division of the Empire which would be accepted by his sons, but he never succeeded in pleasing all three of them. A long series of civil wars, both in his lifetime and after his death, settled the problem only partially. One son took the west and one the east, thus creating the nuclei of the future kingdoms of France and Germany, but the eldest received a long strip of territory stretching from the North Sea to Rome. This middle kingdom included the Low Countries and the Rhineland, Alsace and Lorraine, Switzerland, Savoy, Dauphiné, and Provence, the Po valley, and central Italy. Perhaps it was hoped that the eldest brother, ruling a central territory which included both "capitals" (Rome and Aachen), could preserve some degree of unity in the Empire, but his kingdom never achieved political stability. It soon broke up into smaller states, which in peaceful times had little influence and which in war furnished the battlefields and the spoils for powerful neighbors. The history of Western Europe, from the ninth to the twentieth centuries, has been dominated by the struggle between France and Germany for control of the middle kingdom.

The division of Charlemagne's unwieldy Empire into smaller states might have solved many problems if it could have been accomplished peacefully and irrevocably. But it was done in the heat of conflict and none of the later Carolingians were satisfied with the results. The stronger kings dreamed of reuniting the Empire under their own rule; the weaker ones at least hoped to increase their share. In the frequent wars of the ninth century the counts and other members of the nobility were the only gainers. They furnished the armies with which the Carolingians fought, but they demanded a high price for their aid. By playing one ruler against another and by mutiny and desertion, they extorted grants of land, hereditary countships, and immunity from the authority of the king's representatives. In the turbulent middle zone some of them became petty kings; even in the more stable eastern and western realms they built up semi-independent principalities. By 900 the Carolingians had little direct authority over the kingdoms which they nominally ruled.

To increase the confusion, a new series of invasions struck Europe in the ninth century. Vikings from the North, Magyars from the East, and Moslems from the South plundered the coasts, the plains, and the river valleys. The raiders, who traveled by ship or on horseback, had the advantages of speed and surprise; the bewildered kings were seldom able to concentrate their armies rapidly enough to protect threatened districts. Defense had to be organized on a local basis if it was to be at all effective, and the counts and other great landholders were the obvious leaders of resistance. They raised their own armies; they built castles to protect the open country; they garrisoned the walled towns. Such activities greatly increased their authority over their neighbors and their independence of the central government. In France and in Italy, where the kings had been least successful in repelling the enemy, almost all governmental powers passed into the hands of local lords. In England and Germany, where the kings had a better military record, the growth of lordship was not so spectacular, and the central government retained some authority over local leaders.

The great raids ended during the tenth century, but Europe did not recover immediately from the damage which they had caused. Large areas had been conquered by the invaders; these heathen settlements had to be assimilated or destroyed. The Northmen in England, Ireland, and Normandy accepted Christianity and the western tradition without hesitation, but the Magyars of the Hungarian plain were a more difficult group to absorb. They were not fully converted until the eleventh century and never merged with other peoples as the Northmen did. As for the Moslems, lords of Sicily, Sardinia, and the Balearic islands, they were completely unassimilable, and had to be conquered in a long series of wars. They were not completely expelled from Sicily and Sardinia until the beginning of the twelfth century, and they kept their pirates' nests in the Balearics until the thirteenth century.

The invaders had raided far beyond the area of their conquests and had disrupted normal lines of communication. The Moslems blocked the main land route between France and Italy for years and made navigation in the western Mediterranean extremely hazardous. Forays of the Northmen interrupted travel in the French river valleys, while Magyar horsemen threatened communications between Germany and Italy. The tendency to local self-sufficiency, already strong, was reinforced by the dangers to shipping and travel. No community could be absolutely sure that it would receive supplies from other regions in time of peace, or military assistance in case of war. Society had to be organized so that each district could meet its minimum needs, economic, political, and military, from its own resources. Life was better when outside help was available, but life had to be possible even when outside contacts were reduced to a minimum.

It was in this atmosphere of decaying central authority, civil war, invasion, and economic stagnation that feudalism developed. It was not a system; it was based on no theory; it was an improvisation to meet a desperate emergency. Formed out of materials ready to hand, shaped by dissimilar events and by individuals of varying ability, it could not be uniform, consistent, or logical. It was a means of preserving the rudiments of social organization in a period of confusion, a way of getting the essential work of government done on a local basis when larger political units had proved ineffectual. Essentially it was the rule of bosses (or lords) and their gangs (or vassals). Strong men surrounded by groups of armed retainers took over the government of relatively small districts, and supplied the armed forces and ran the courts which protected their subjects against external and internal enemies.

Scholars have argued for generations over the origins of feudalism, and are still far from agreement on many points. This much seems certain, that the local lord—the great man of the township or the county—appears at the very dawn of European history. Rich in land and in cattle, protector of his people, chief of the warriors of his community, he is known to the early Italians and Celts as well as to the primitive Germans. The Roman government had curtailed the military and political power of the local magnates, but had not destroyed their influence and prestige; the Germans, with no bureaucratic state to take on the work of local government, had preserved the old system of chiefs and retainers. The German occupation of the Western Empire naturally strengthened the ancient tradition of local lordship. Remnants of Roman ideas and Roman methods of government acted as a restraining influence for a while, but withered away from lack of direction by the kings and lack of support by their subjects. When the Carolingians came to power, local magnates were far stronger than the weak Frankish kings of the earlier dynasty. They obeyed royal orders only when it pleased them and frequently rebelled against unpopular mayors of the palace. They had almost complete control over the men who lived on their lands, but they took little responsibility for governing them.

The Carolingians recognized these facts, and adjusted their government to them. They could not destroy the power of the local lords; they could hope to use it for their own purposes. Since the magnates controlled the best fighting men, they were asked to bring their troops to the royal army and to act as commanders of the free men of their districts. Since the idea of lordship had destroyed the Roman concept of obedience to administrative agents sent out by the central government, the Carolingians ordered all men to choose a lord. The Carolingians themselves were to be the supreme lords, and thus a hierarchy of personal relationships between lord and man was to replace the old bureaucratic hierarchy of ruler, provincial governor, local administrator, and subjects.

This Carolingian system was buttressed by the bishops and the counts. The bishops owed their offices to the kings and usually gave them effective support. The counts, though they were chosen from the richest and most noble families, had not yet made their positions hereditary and could hope to gain greater power and wealth by supporting the kings. But the growing disorder in the Carolingian realms gradually weakened the loyalty of both ruling groups. The bishops, on the whole, tried to preserve the Carolingian state, but were slowly forced to look for protection to local magnates. The counts, who had always had tendencies toward independence, took full advantage of the confusion caused by civil war and invasion. They first made their offices hereditary, and then set themselves up as practically autonomous rulers of the regions where they were strong.

The long chain of lordship, reaching from the king through the counts to the local magnates and ordinary freemen, was beginning to break. The breaks did not always come at the same place and some links in the chain held in spite of the terrible strain which they endured. This meant that feudalism did not have the same structure in all parts of the Carolingian realms and that not all regions were completely feudalized. Generally speaking, the process was most complete and most logical in the part of France north of the Loire. There the counts gained practical independence of the king while keeping control of most of their subordinates. Able and aggressive counts then attacked their neighbors and built up large feudal states composed of many counties. Southern France was more chaotic. Many lesser landowners never became involved in feudal relationships and the great counts never succeeded in gaining control over all the lesser lords. The hilly region of the Massif Central was especially disorderly; there the owner of a small castle might rule a few square miles without worrying about any superior. In Germany the king retained more control over great men and great offices than was the case in France; in Italy, as in southern France, the process of feudalization was uneven and incomplete. England, outside the Carolingian sphere, escaped feudalism until the Norman Conquest, when the northern French feudal pattern was imposed on the country.

Yet, with all these differences, two facts stand out. No matter what the degree of feudalization, it never resulted in pure anarchy. There was always some government left, whether it was that of a king, or a great count, or a petty baron. It was government reduced to the barest minimum, which was usually inefficient and often unjust. But courts were held and frontiers were defended even in the most disorderly parts of Europe; there never was a time or place in which each individual fighting man was a law to himself. In the second place, no matter what the degree of feudalization, effective government was local government. Even in Germany, where the king remained fairly strong, even in the great counties of northern France where lesser lords remained relatively loyal to their superiors, the average man sought justice and protection from the local magnate, not from more distant authorities. The local court was his government and the local castle his refuge.

It is difficult to see how this loose feudal organization ever became the basis for the tightly organized modern state-system, how a society based on war became a society based on law. Yet the facts are there. The two best governed and most prosperous states of the early modern period, England and France, rose in regions which had been thoroughly feudalized. Germany and Italy, much less feudalized, were also much slower to develop adequate political systems. Clearly feudalism was not a blight which prevented the growth of more elaborate types of organization; one might even argue that it had a stimulating effect upon political growth.

In the first place, the facts of feudal political life never corresponded to prevailing political theory. Men who thought at all about politics never believed that the small feudal principality was a satisfactory or sufficient unit; they continued to talk of kingdoms and of empires. The universal church found it difficult to remain universal in an atmosphere of feudal division; its great influence, for many generations, was on the side of larger political units. The feudal lords themselves, through tradition or necessity, acknowledged the theoretical supremacy of their kings. These beliefs and theories had at first little influence, but they did create a climate of opinion which improved the chances for political integration. A king who protected distant subjects against their immediate lords, who enforced a ruling of his court against a recalcitrant baron, who used a flimsy excuse to annex a feudal principality to his own domain, was not treated as an outside aggressor. His rights were unquestioned. If he could enforce them, everyone usually acquiesced in the results.

In the second place, feudal government itself was far more flexible, far less hostile to experiment than is usually realized. It was, to repeat, an improvisation, neither planned in advance nor bound by rules. The lord preserved some old institutions, but he was quite free to abandon them or to modify them if he found it necessary. The one essential element in feudal government was the court in which the lord met with his principal vassals, a body which was a tribunal, a legislature, and an executive council all in one. Feudal courts worked out their basic rules of law and procedure by solving individual problems as they arose. They were free to experiment, to mix their principles with large doses of expediency, to adjust their general concepts of right and wrong to local conditions. Not all feudal governments were successful in developing new institutions, but the best of them proved surprisingly fertile. The principal departments of government of the French and English monarchies grew out of feudal courts. The Anglo-American system of common law is based on the feudal law of the court of the king of England.

In the third place, feudal government had some success in gaining the loyalty of the people. This was important; the Roman Empire had fallen because it lacked that loyalty, and the Carolingian Empire was weak because, in the end, it was supported only by the Church. Feudal government was local government. It was on a scale which corresponded to the experience and interests of its subjects. It was based on personal allegiance to a visible and nearby lord, not on allegiance to a remote and abstract authority. Both the Roman and the Carolingian Empires had been too large to mean much to the ordinary man; the work of a feudal government concerned him directly. Therefore we find occasional devotion to the feudal ruler, and almost always loyalty to the administrative and legal customs of the feudal state. They formed part of the birthright of the people; the fact that they were worked out to fit local conditions made them strike deep roots in local soil. It is also true that early feudal government was government reduced to a minimum and that the most common criticism of such a government was that it did not do enough. The combination of loyalty to the local government and desire for stronger government was one of the factors which made possible the experimentation and development of new political techniques which have already been mentioned.

Finally, the relation between lord and vassal changed rapidly during the feudal centuries. At first the vassal was primarily a fighting man, not a landed proprietor. He was often a member of his lord's household; even when he received a grant of land (fief) in return for his services he was expected to spend most of his time at the lord's court. Vassals of this type had no special reason to be interested in good government or the rule of law; they profited from their lord's victories, not from his administration of justice. But this strict, early form of vassalage was soon contaminated. Great men became vassals; their service could not be made frequent or burdensome, and so all service tended to be reduced. Lesser vassals soon received fiefs as a matter of right, not favor; the landless vassal, common enough in the ninth century, was rare after 1100. The vassal with land acquired the mentality of a landlord; he became more interested in preserving his estate than in fighting for his superiors. The lords found it more difficult to make war because their vassals tried to limit the amount of service which they rendered. In many regions the rule was established that vassals owed only forty days of service a year at their own expense. There was also a tendency to limit free service to defensive operations; vassals claimed that they owed no service outside the district which their lord ruled. But as the chances for conquests decreased, the chances to make a profit out of good government increased. Lesser vassals and minor lords were eager to gain protection for their lands; they were good customers for the new legal techniques developed by feudal courts. A ruler who suppressed disorder and encouraged peaceful settlement of disputes was sure of gaining wide support—not only from the common people, who had little political influence, but also from the old military class, which was becoming a class of country gentlemen.

II. THE REVIVAL OF THE EMPIRE—
GERMANY AND ITALY

No part of Europe escaped invasion and civil war in the century after Charlemagne's death, but Germany suffered less damage than the other Carolingian realms. A poorer country than France or Italy, it was not so attractive to invaders. The specialized fighting class of vassals had not yet taken over responsibility for military operations, so that it was easier to raise an army in Germany. German peasants could still be used as soldiers and German kings were better generals than their relatives in France and Italy. The invading peoples suffered heavy losses in their conflicts with the Germans. Viking raids almost ceased after a great battle in 891 and the Magyars caused little trouble after their army was almost annihilated by King Otto in 955. German rulers were equally successful in civil war. They succeeded, in spite of the opposition of the French king, in annexing most of the middle kingdom (the Low

Countries, Luxemburg, Alsace, Lorraine, and the Rhône valley) so that the German frontier ran 50 to 100 miles west of its present position. They suppressed most of the rebellions in their own country and stunted the growth of German feudalism. Lordship and vassalage were not unknown in Germany, and public offices tended to become hereditary in certain families. Yet dukes and counts were still royal officials and could be dismissed for disobedience. By the tenth century Germany was probably the best-governed and certainly the most powerful country in Western Europe.

The peak of German power came in the reign of Otto I (936–973), a member of the Saxon dynasty which had replaced the childless eastern Carolingians. Otto was in such a strong position that he could expand his political power in almost any direction—against the disorderly French kingdom in the west, against the loosely organized Slavic principalities in the east, or against the headless kingdom of Italy in the south. The only danger was that he would dissipate his strength by reaching for too much—and Otto did not entirely escape this pitfall. He restrained himself in the case of France, intervening just enough to keep his friends there in power. But he tried to acquire both Italy and the Slavic border lands, and for this he has been judged harshly by many historians.

The case against him is easy to state. Germany did not have the resources both to dominate Italy and to occupy the lands of the Slavs. The Italian involvement was useless, since the Germans never gained permanent control of the country, and dangerous, because it aroused the jealousy of all other rulers. Expansion to the east was both permanent and profitable, but the movement should have been kept under royal control. Italian problems made it impossible for the central government to watch closely the eastern frontier; therefore the political profits of the drive to the east went to the princes and not to the king. The examples of Spain and the United States show the unwisdom of Otto's policy. Both countries had long, open frontiers during their formative periods;

both countries had to conquer and settle much of their present-day territory. But while the Spaniards were reconquering the Iberian peninsula from the Moors, while the Americans were driving through Indian territories to the Pacific, both peoples avoided political entanglements elsewhere. The frontier districts were kept under control; strong central governments were established, and both countries were able to play a great rôle in international affairs after they had reached their limits of expansion.

It is easy for us to reason this way, but it is a little unfair to condemn Otto for not having the wisdom of a thousand years of hindsight. He was not entirely a free agent as far as Italy was concerned; that turbulent country was begging for foreign intervention. The legitimate line of Carolingian kings had long since disappeared, and the factions of nobles who were trying to control the kingdom were actively seeking foreign aid. It would have complicated Otto's task of keeping control of Germany if one of his dukes or a French count had become ruler of the Po valley. Moreover Otto, though no Carolingian, was trying to preserve the Carolingian tradition of government in Germany. Like Charlemagne, he relied heavily on an alliance with the Church; like Charlemagne, he used bishops and abbots as advisers and administrators. This close connection with the Church must have turned his thoughts toward Rome.

Otto's intervention in Italy was decisive. He was recognized as king by the north Italians and was crowned emperor by the pope in 962. The imperial title had meant little after the death of Charlemagne's son, Louis the Pious, and even the title had disappeared after 924. Now it was revived for the benefit of a king of Germany, and for almost nine centuries German rulers were to claim the title of Roman emperor. This Ottonian Empire was to be a real force in Europe for a much longer period than the Carolingian Empire, because Otto had many able successors while Charlemagne had none. It is also true that the revival of the Empire satisfied the psychological needs of many medieval men. It was a symbol of unity and order in a world which lacked both qualities. But Otto and his successors wanted to rule more than a symbol; they wanted their Empire to be a reality. This meant that they had to continue their efforts to control north Italy and to protect Rome and the pope. Thus Otto's involvement in Italy, which might have been temporary, became permanent, and his policy of alliance with the Church became an absolute necessity. Italy could not be held, the imperial title could not be acquired, without the friendship of the pope. So Otto's successors were condemned to endless journeys across the Alps and permanent intervention in Italian and papal politics.

The immediate consequences were not bad. For a century after Otto's death Germany remained strong and united in a disorganized and apparently disintegrating Europe. Neither the lack of direct heirs to the throne nor the rebellions of the great men shook the stability of the German monarchy. When two successive emperors died without heirs the crown was transferred without difficulty to a collateral branch of the royal family. When the dukes rebelled, as they did periodically, the risings were suppressed without great difficulty. Feudalism was no problem, except in the regions bordering on France. Yet Germany was not quite as well off as it seemed. For one thing, the drive east against the Slavs was not going smoothly; great advances were followed by almost equally great setbacks. Even more important, Germany was not creating new institutions to parallel those which were growing up in the feudal West. The government was still basically a Carolingian government. It depended on the voluntary co-operation of the great men, of the prelates and magnates. With some exaggeration, we can say that the king had no lands, no income, and no army of his own; if the great men were to withdraw their support he was helpless. He relied especially on the backing of the Church; the monasteries provided much of his income, the bishops supplied many of his troops, and his most loyal and capable officials were churchmen. Thus a quarrel with the Church would greatly weaken him and so give the lay lords a chance to gain their independence.

The materials for such a quarrel were being assembled in the middle years of the eleventh century. It started, innocently enough, with a reform movement in the monasteries which set new standards of morality and asceticism for the clergy. German rulers at first saw no danger in this program; indeed, they gave it active encouragement. After all, a reformed monastery was not only a more godly place, but was also apt to be more solvent. Thus by aiding reform the emperor piled up spiritual credits in heaven and temporal credits in the monasteries, and he expected both to be available to him in his hour of need. Reform gave such excellent results in the monasteries that the emperor was willing to encourage it in other organs of the Church, and especially in the papacy. Ever since the revival of the Empire in 962 the popes had been, with one or two exceptions, an undistinguished lot, selected either by the Roman nobility or by the emperor. The reform movement had not gained full control of the papal court; it had been just strong enough to cause conflict between reformers and conservatives which led to a confused set of elections. As a result three men were claiming the title of pope in 1046. The emperor Henry III, full of zeal for reform and conscious of his responsibility as temporal head of the Christian world, found this intolerable. He secured the resignation or deposition of all three claimants and imposed his own choice, a German bishop of excellent morals and great ability. This man, Leo IX, began a series of reforming popes who greatly increased the power and prestige of their office.

Henry III had not feared a strong, reform-minded pope, for it had been long since the West had seen a pope who was a real leader. Potentially the papal office was the greatest in Western Europe; actually only a few popes had realized its possibilities. As spiritual head of Christendom, as the donor of the imperial crown, the pope might acquire greater prestige than the emperor; as administrative head of the Church he might have as much actual power. And the old slogans of the reformers, as reinterpreted by the popes of the latter half of the eleventh century, began to have ominous meanings for the Empire. Churchmen were to be free from all lay control and all worldly involvements. This meant freedom not only from petty feudal lords (with this the emperor heartily agreed) but from the emperor himself. He was to lose his power of intervening in papal elections; the pope was now to be chosen by a college of cardinals. He was to lose his power of appointing and investing bishops; they were no longer to consider themselves primarily officials of the Empire and servants of the king. They were now to devote themselves to the service of the Church and the pope; their work for secular rulers could be only incidental and intermittent.

Such a policy was bound to cause trouble. The Empire and the German kingdom, which was the real heart of the Empire, depended absolutely on the support of the clergy. If the emperor could not appoint bishops and abbots, if he could not be sure of their loyalty, if he could not use them as his agents, his whole system of government was wrecked. And yet the reformers had a strong case; the Church was not created to serve the state, and men of religion should be subject only to religious authority. Compromise would have been difficult in any case; it was made almost impossible by accidents of personality. Henry III, who had been widely respected, died prematurely, and his heir, Henry IV, was only six when he came to the throne. During his long minority the lay magnates in Germany became more independent while the reformers consolidated their position at the papal court. When Henry IV came of age he was eager to repair the damage done during his minority and to restore the prestige of the Empire. Like many other men who became kings as boys, he had exaggerated ideas of his own power and wanted quick solutions to all his problems. Just as he began to develop his program for Germany, one of the outstanding leaders of the reform party was elected pope. Gregory VII (1073–1085), though a much older man, re-sembled Henry in his unwillingness to compromise and his desire to obtain quick results. He wanted the pope to be recognized, not only as administrative head of the Church but as leader of the whole Christian community. The pope was to be the final and supreme authority in Europe; the clergy, his agents, were to be freed im-mediately from all lay control.

When Gregory began to apply these principles in north Italy and Germany, Henry tried to have him deposed by the German bishops. But Gregory had allies—the princes of the Empire, who were irritated by Henry's strenuous attempts to reassert royal power. They saw that freedom for the Church meant freedom for them too, and when Henry was excommunicated by the pope they withdrew their allegiance from him. Henry's position was des-perate, for Gregory and the princes planned to depose him at a great council to be held in Germany. Henry had to prevent this meeting at all costs. He slipped across the Alps with a small escort, intercepted Gregory at the castle of Canossa, and begged for absolution. Gregory, as a Christian priest, could not reject a penitent sinner, even though he knew that his act would weaken his position in Germany. He made the reconciliation as dramatic as possible: Henry had to stand in penitent's garb outside the castle for three days and was then forced to subject his quarrel with the princes to the pope's judgment, but in the end he was absolved. With the pope, for the moment, neutralized, Henry could meet the German rebels on equal terms. He had saved his crown, at the price of personal humiliation.

Canossa was far from being a complete victory for Gregory. The German magnates felt that they had been deserted; the pope's assertions that he was still on their side were discounted, and many of them returned to Henry's party. The king slowly regained control of Germany, and in 1084 was strong enough to drive Gregory out of Rome. Henry was crowned emperor by an anti-pope, and the next year Gregory died in exile. But Henry's victory was even less complete and more fleeting than Gregory's. Succeeding popes continued the struggle; rebellion followed rebellion in Germany, and finally Henry's own son joined the opposition and deposed his father. Henry died the next year, in 1106, powerless and friendless.

The fact that both Henry and Gregory seemed defeated when they died might suggest that the long struggle ended in a stalemate. Actually, the papacy had won a great, though incomplete, victory. The popes had gained their independence from lay authority; neither Italian nobles nor German kings henceforth determined their election. The popes had mobilized the opinion of the Christian world against the most powerful ruler in Europe; they had permanently weakened the great German kingdom. They had shown that it was dangerous to oppose the Church, that military defeats could not permanently thwart, much less destroy, spiritual power. They had not gained as much for the bishops and abbots as they had for themselves; lay rulers still had much to say about the choice of prelates in their districts, and the clergy still bore heavy responsibilities in lay government. But at least it was now recognized that the clergy had two masters; their unquestioning loyalty to a lay ruler could no longer be assumed, and no lay government could rely entirely on their support. The results of this change were especially noticeable in Germany, because German kings, more than any other rulers, had relied on the financial and military aid given by their clergy. When they were no longer sure of this support they lost effective control of their kingdom. Feudalism, which had started late and developed slowly in Germany, now grew rapidly; the great men of the kingdom became almost independent princes. It is true that the twelfth-century kings of Germany, by untiring efforts and skillful diplomacy, managed to prevent complete disruption of their realm. They could, at times, use the clergy against over-powerful lay lords; they could play one group of princes against another or lesser against greater vassals. But this perpetual balancing trick was a strain on everyone, and left the king with no solid base of authority. Germany was less united and therefore less of a factor in European politics in the twelfth century than it had been earlier.

III. THE RENEWAL OF WESTERN CIVILIZATION

The political failure of the Carolingian Empire, and of the German Roman Empire which was its successor, did not mean that Western Europe sank back into complete barbarism almost as soon as it became a distinct and separate cultural entity. It suffered severely from internal wars and external raids; many districts were misgoverned or ungoverned as rulers cracked under the strain and became mere predatory animals. Yet there were always islands of relative security in the sea of disorder. The great century of the Anglo-Saxon kingdom coincided with the worst period of feudal warfare in France; the German Empire was at the height of its power when Italy was split into quarreling fragments. Learning survived, and with learning the memories of a happier and more prosperous society. The people of Europe did not have to discover, for the first time, the benefits of a better social organization. They knew, at least by tradition, what those benefits were; they wanted to regain them; the problem was how to secure the degree of co-operation and organization which would make possible a better life.

Somehow, during the hard years of the tenth and eleventh centuries, they learned again the secret of working together effectively for the common welfare. There is no entirely satisfactory way to explain how they regained this ability, any more than there is a completely satisfactory explanation of why they lost it in the period of the Late Roman Empire. But the reversal is plain to see. From the Late Empire, through the barbarian kingdoms and the Carolingian Empire into early feudalism, every attempt to integrate large numbers of people had failed. The effective units of co-operation were pitifully small—the agricultural community of a few hundred inhabitants, the military community of the lord and a few score followers. Co-operation beyond this level was precarious and impermanent, easily disturbed by individual whims, easily broken by the first shock of adversity. Now, slowly and painfully, the people of Europe began to form larger social units. It could not be done all at once; in some regions it could not be done at all. But by the twelfth century the period of beginnings, which is always the hardest, was over, and Europe had started to develop a high civilization of its own.

The fact that no complete explanation of the change can be given does not mean that it is altogether a mystery. Three lines of inquiry seem promising—the political developments associated with the maturing of feudalism, the religious developments associated with the reform movement in the Church, and the economic developments associated with the growth of towns and the increase in commerce. No one of these has priority, either in time or in importance; they were closely associated and each stimulated the others. If political developments are discussed first, it is only because some foundation for this discussion was laid in the last sections.

Feudal government, as we saw earlier, was flexible and adaptable. It could be adjusted easily to fit local conditions, and under favorable conditions it generated new institutions with surprising rapidity. The greater feudal lords were not inclined to give their vassals an entirely free hand. They disliked private wars because a series of small victories might make a petty vassal too strong. They disliked leaving all local authority in the possession of a vassal because his subjects might then forget that he had a superior. To keep their vassals in check they often fortified strategic positions throughout their territories and left them in charge of a deputy who was to hold a court and collect revenue in the name of the suzerain. When this occurred, the feudal lordship began to change into a feudal state.

The most successful of these feudal states were Flanders and

Normandy on the north coast of France. As they became more peaceful and orderly their population began to grow, and younger sons had to emigrate in order to find a livelihood. Flemish expansion, on the whole, was peaceful, although the counts of Flanders persistently tried to annex small lordships along their frontiers. But the greater part of the surplus Flemish population sought economic rather than political conquests. They drained swamps and ocean marshes in the Low Countries; they migrated to England where there was plenty of unoccupied land; they moved to the eastern frontier of Germany and settled on lands which the German lords had taken from the Slavs. Others found opportunities in the rapidly growing industrial towns of Flanders, which became the largest in Northern Europe.

Norman expansion was more warlike. Scattered bands of Norman adventurers began to move to southern Italy in the 1020's and 1030's. This was ideal country for tough and ambitious fighters, since it was being disputed by local princes, Moslem raiders from Sicily, and generals sent out from Constantinople to retain the last foothold of the Eastern Empire in the West. At first the Normans hired out to the highest bidder, but soon they began to operate on their own account. By the middle of the century they had established a strong principality; by 1071 they had possession of all the southern part of the peninsula. Meanwhile a great Norman leader, Count Roger, had begun the conquest of Sicily. The Moslems, who had held it for generations, resisted fiercely, but by 1091 their last stronghold was taken. Early in the next century the Norman principalities were united into a kingdom of Sicily which was one of the most centralized and best-governed states in Europe.

The Norman conquest of England was accomplished more quickly than was the conquest of southern Italy because it was an official project of Duke William, instead of the venture of a few poor knights. England was an attractive field of expansion for an ambitious ruler; it was fertile, thinly populated, and militarily weak. England had avoided feudalism and the internal wars which accompanied it, but in avoiding feudalism the English had avoided modernizing their army. The feudal army, with its backbone of heavy-armed knights, was unbeatable during the eleventh century; it had the best equipment and the newest tactics. No other military organization was as effective; seasoned Viking and Saracen raiders, disciplined Byzantine regiments, Arab horsemen of the East, and wild tribal levies of the West all went down to defeat before the heavy-armed knights. The English army was brave and experienced; in the very year of the conquest it repulsed a Norse invader with great losses, but it was no match for William and his knights. The Normans won a complete victory at Hastings and William was accepted as king of the English.

England had gained unity in a long struggle against invading Northmen, and with unity had developed a remarkable system of local government. The country was divided into shires (or counties) and each shire was governed by a shire-reeve (or sheriff) on behalf of the king. The fact that this is still the basic system of local government in some parts of the United States shows the strength and value of the system. But although Anglo-Saxon England was better governed than many parts of the continent, it had serious weaknesses. Lordship was growing; the great landed proprietors were gaining more and more power over the peasants and were beginning to stand between them and the government. The earls who had general supervision of large sections of the country were becoming rebellious and independent. The government had no very good way of controlling either great landlords or earls. They had no fiefs which could be confiscated for political misbehavior and it was difficult to deprive them of offices or local leadership without making war on them. England, in many ways, was in the same situation as Germany. An old system of government was beginning to weaken under new strains; a monarchy based on the support of the great office- and land-holders was threatened as these men became independent, territorial lords.

The quarrel with the Church made it impossible to stop the slow disintegration of Germany, but the decay of the old English monarchy was halted by the Norman Conquest. William preserved all the powers of an Anglo-Saxon king and added to them the strength of a supreme feudal lord. The great men now held lands and political power from him as fiefs; if they disobeyed, their fiefs were confiscated. Enough vassals always remained loyal to the king to enable him to enforce his orders; no English feudal lord ever became an independent prince. England remained united and relatively peaceful, one of the best-governed regions in Western Europe.

Flanders and Normandy, England and Sicily were outstanding political successes, but they were not unique. Everywhere, as the invasions ceased, as feudal lords reached the limits of easy conquest, there was a little less disorder, a little more security. The stronger French feudal lords kept order in their own lands, even if they attacked their neighbors. Germany was relatively well governed until the great struggle with the Church. In places where the rulers were unable to improve conditions the Church took the initiative. Peace associations—something like the vigilantes of our old West —were formed under the leadership of the clergy. Members of these associations swore to prevent crimes of violence and to protect non-combatants in time of war. They were especially effective, where they were backed by a strong feudal lord, but even without this backing they put some restraint on the endless violence of the military class.

The increase in security was slow, and in some places almost imperceptible. Yet even a slight increase could have momentous consequences. Europe had sunk to a bare subsistence level during the period of invasion and civil war—it had no surplus food, labor, or energy. A little increase in security could create very large surpluses—for example, there is evidence that population grew rapidly in every region where some political stability was gained. The tough and frugal communities which survived the difficult years of the ninth and tenth centuries needed only a little encouragement to release tremendous energies. Europe in 1100 was not very orderly or law-abiding by our standards, but it was so much better than it had been that co-operation on a large scale was once more possible.

A religious revival accompanied and stimulated the political revival. The importance of this movement is easily overlooked, but it is one of the most significant developments of this transitional period. Europe had been nominally Christian since the Late Roman Empire, but the intensity of religious conviction was at first not very great. Barbarians who had been converted *en masse* and country-dwellers who seldom saw a priest were not much influenced by the teachings of the Church. The establishment of a parish system, which brought everyone into regular and frequent contact with the clergy, was the answer to these difficulties, but the parish system spread slowly, and was not fully established until the Carolingian period. Then the ninth-century invasions brought in new barbarians, and destroyed parish churches in many places. As a result, it was not until the late tenth century that the Church had steady, uninterrupted contact with most of the people of Western Europe, and it was only then that Christianity began to exert its full effect on Western men. It got under their skins; it was no longer a matter of external forms and ceremonies, but a matter of personal conviction. People began to worry more about making their behavior conform to Christian standards; they were more willing to follow the leadership of the Church.

We have already seen several examples of this new intensity of religious conviction. The reform movement in the Church, which attempted to free the clergy from worldly ties, could never have succeeded without popular support. The German emperors were forced to yield much of their control over the Church because public opinion turned against them. The peace movement, which attempted to suppress or mitigate the senseless violence of feudal war, was led by churchmen, but would have had no strength without the support of laymen of all classes. There was a great increase in gifts to churches and monasteries, and an equally large increase in the number of people taking religious vows. The old established monasteries were no longer strict enough to satisfy some of the converts; new orders were founded which made greater demands on their members. The first great reformed order was that of Cluny, founded in 910. With hundreds of monasteries scattered through Europe, it played an important rôle in the eleventh-century quarrel between Church and Empire. Later came the Carthusians, who lived as hermits in isolated cells and met only for religious services. The Cistercians, founded at the end of the eleventh century, refused to own serfs, and cleared waste land with their own hands. Fervor and piety gave the new orders great prestige; the most influential men in the West during the late eleventh and early twelfth centuries were the abbots of the great reformed monasteries.

The most spectacular result of the religious revival was the First Crusade. It was a demonstration of papal leadership, a manifestation of popular piety, and an indication of the growing self-confidence of Western Europe. Europe no longer waited in anguish for an attack from outside enemies. Now, for the first time, it took the initiative and sent its armies far into the lands of two great Eastern civilizations. It took courage to do this, and the courage was based on the absolute conviction that the Crusade was the will of God.

We shall never know with certainty why Pope Urban II proclaimed the Crusade at Clermont in 1095. Many things distressed him, and the Crusade was a solution to many of his problems. Doctrinal disputes and pressure from rebellious Turkish mercenaries had broken the Moslem caliphate into a group of quarreling states, and access to Jerusalem was no longer as easy for Christian pilgrims as it had been in the days of the great caliphs. A military expedition could take advantage of the fragmentation of Moslem

power and end the scandal of infidel domination of the Holy
Places. The Eastern Church had broken with Rome in 1054 and
the Eastern Empire had been badly defeated by the Turks at Man-
zikert in 1071. A military expedition could strengthen the Byzantine bulwark, thus giving protection to the West, and the Eastern
Emperor might show his gratitude by urging the reunion of the
two Churches. In the West the struggle with Henry IV was still
going on, and the German ruler was having considerable success
in Italy. The Crusade could add to papal prestige; it could prove
that the pope, not the emperor, was the leader of Western Christendom. Finally, it should not be forgotten that the Council of
Clermont began with a discussion of the peace movement and that
the Crusade had a very direct connection with the peace movement: it removed a large number of quarrelsome men from
Europe.

Whatever the pope's calculations, the response to his appeal was
based largely on simple piety. The Crusade was the greatest of all
pilgrimages, the most efficacious of all penances, and most Crusaders sought only spiritual benefits from the expedition. If a mere
visit to Jerusalem were sufficient penance for the deepest sins,
how much greater the reward for those who freed the Holy
Places from infidel domination. Even the feudal adventurers who
joined the Crusade hoping for lands and booty were not immune
to these ideas. They gained their lands, but they too made the
pilgrimage to the Holy Sepulchre and bathed in the waters of
Jordan.

The Crusaders needed intense faith to attain their objective.
Almost everything else was against them—their ignorance of the
geography and politics of the Near East, their lack of experience
in organizing large armies, their suspicions of each other and of
their nominal allies, the Orthodox Christians of the East. The first
Crusaders who reached Asia Minor—mostly unarmed pilgrims
guarded by a handful of poor knights—were massacred by the
Turks. The real armies, led by the great lords of France, western

Germany, and Norman Italy, were not quite so helpless, but they suffered severely during the long years of fighting and marching. They were almost defeated by the Turks in crossing Asia Minor; they almost starved during the siege of the great fortress city of Antioch. They were saved by the fact that the heavily armed Western soldiers were invincible when they had anything like decent leadership, and by the sharp divisions among their opponents. A decisive victory over a Moslem army at Antioch opened the way to Jerusalem, and the Holy City fell to the Crusaders in July 1099—almost four years after the Council of Clermont and three years after the main armies had started their journey to the East.

The success of the Crusade had a tremendous moral effect on Europe. There were already some reasons for optimism, but they were based on small, local, unspectacular gains. Now an almost impossible task had been accomplished, and everyone in Europe was aware of it. God had set them the task, and God had given them the strength to perform it. It is not surprising that there was an increase in confidence, in self-assurance, in optimism in twelfth-century Europe.

Even more important, the successful Crusade, following the successful reform movement and the successful struggle with the Empire, firmly established the leadership of the Church. From the late eleventh well into the thirteenth century, the Church set the goals and fixed the standards for Western European society. This was leadership and not dictatorship; the Church did not and could not control all secular interests and activities. Loyalty to the Church was like patriotism today; it was taken for granted, and therefore ignored, in the ordinary transactions of daily life. Men were selfish in the Middle Ages as they are selfish now; they sought power and profit for themselves without considering the general welfare. But, just as the most corrupt politician or predatory business man of today can hardly defy openly the national interest, so the barons and the townsmen of the Middle Ages found

it difficult to defy the Church. They had to conform, at least out-
wardly; they could not pursue indefinitely lines of conduct which
the Church condemned. And the completely selfish man was rare,
then as now. Most people had some tincture of religious idealism,
some generous impulses which they followed occasionally. They
accepted the leadership of the Church, not because they feared
hell, but because it made them feel better when they conformed
to the ideals of their society. By conforming they could overcome
their feeling of personal insignificance; they could become fellow-
workers in the divine plan for the world. The leadership of the
Church was accepted because it gave meaning to life. And it was
because they had leadership and were sure that life had meaning
that men of the twelfth century could achieve so much.

The political revival had given the people of Western Europe a
little more security; the religious revival had given them consid-
erably more confidence. It is not surprising, under these conditions, that there was an economic revival. As we have already seen,
increased security allowed an increase in population and in agricultural production. The effects were cumulative, for most of the
surplus population was put to work clearing new land for cultivation. All over Europe forests were cut down, marshes drained,
lands reclaimed from the sea. In every region hundreds of new
agricultural settlements were formed, as the Newtons and Vil-
leneuves and Neustadts scattered over the map of Europe still
testify. As a result, Europe now had an overall agricultural surplus,
which could be used to support a growing urban population.

Commerce and industry were also developing at a rapid
rate. Moslem disunity, which had made possible the success of the
First Crusade, had also made possible a revival of Western sea-
power. The Norman conquest of Sicily opened the passage between the western and eastern Mediterranean basins. Pisa and
Genoa developed strong fleets which cleared European waters of
Moslem raiders and even attacked Arab strongholds on the Afri-

can coast. A Genoese fleet was of great assistance to the First Crusade in the march from Antioch to Jerusalem. The Mediterranean had never been closed to Christian ships, but after 1100 it was far safer to send large fleets to the East. Imports of oriental goods greatly increased, and the Italian cities which were the chief importers grew in wealth and population. Their growth, in turn, had stimulating effects on towns beyond the Alps. Oriental goods had to be distributed through Europe, and the caravans of wandering merchants had to find secure places in which to display and store their wares. So the little fortified burgs of North Europe, which had been merely ecclesiastical and administrative centers, acquired a population of traders and carriers and developed active commercial life. Artisans naturally flocked to these centers of population and built up local trade, which in many towns became more important than the international trade in eastern goods.

Meanwhile a great industrial development was taking place in Flanders, which complemented the commercial development of Italy. As we have seen, Flanders had a surplus population. It also had much waste land, suitable only for grazing, and an ideal climate for wool-working. Flemish cloth was prized at least as early as the time of Charlemagne, and by the end of the eleventh century it was being sold all through Europe and even in the East. The great Flemish cloth-towns, such as Ghent and Bruges, grew rapidly and were second only to the Italian seaports in wealth and population. The cloth trade, like the trade in oriental goods, stimulated the growth of towns all along the main routes of commerce, especially after Flemings and Italians established active business relationships.

By 1100 towns were becoming important in the social and economic life of Europe. The total urban population was still not very large, certainly less than ten per cent of that of Europe as a whole, but its influence could not be measured by numbers alone. The mere existence of communities of merchants and manufacturers created problems which could not be solved by the old forms of organization. A feudal court, which could deal fairly well with cases involving land tenure, was incompetent in matters of commercial law. No merchant could thrive if he were treated like a subject peasant. Personal freedom and a certain amount of local self-government were absolutely essential if the towns were to prosper. The wiser lords granted these privileges without too much reluctance because they saw that they could obtain larger income from prosperous towns. Less enlightened rulers, who tried to keep the townsmen down, were faced with endless revolts, and often had to make the same concessions in the end. Thus the townsmen, as a whole, became a privileged class, less favored than the nobility and clergy, but far above the ordinary peasant.

Even more important, the influence of the towns and the growth of trade tended to weaken the old agricultural system of Europe. As long as each village had to be largely self-sufficient, as long as there were no extensive markets for agricultural products, the organization inherited from the Romans and modified in the early Middle Ages was not capable of much improvement. Each peasant had a share of the land of his village, and rights of pasture and wood-cutting in waste and forest. The fields were cultivated by pooling all the animal and human labor of the village, since few men had enough oxen, or enough tools to do the work by themselves. The lord had a large share of the land, which the villagers cultivated for him; he also received a portion of the produce of each peasant as rent. Some peasants were serfs, which meant that they had smaller holdings and worked more for the lord than the freemen did. But even the free peasants were heavily burdened with dues and community obligations. The serfs were bound to their lord and were not supposed to leave his lands without his permission. But in a period of great insecurity and little opportunity this was not a particularly galling restriction. Most men remained all their lives in the community in which they were born, since it was the only place in which they could hope to make a living. The medieval village was organized for survival, not for the production of salable surpluses. If everyone did his job, if weather, or plague, or war did not destroy the crops or wipe out the workers, there would be enough food for the community. That was as much as anyone could hope for in the troubled years of the ninth and tenth centuries.

The economic revival slowly, but steadily, changed this pattern. As new land was brought into cultivation, as urban population increased, the peasants found opportunities to improve their condition. Clearing new land was difficult work; no peasant would undertake it unless he were given special inducements. Rents had to be cut sharply and labor services almost eliminated. The towns, as we have seen, secured guarantees of personal freedom for their inhabitants. Gradually the rule became established that residence in a town for a year and a day guaranteed freedom for any peasant. These facts, in turn, had repercussions on the older villages. If a peasant could secure new land on easy terms by running away to a clearing or draining project, if he could secure personal freedom by running away to a town, then lords who demanded heavy services and rents were going to lose many of their tenants. In areas where the demand for labor was great, the position of the peasants improved rapidly. Services were reduced or commuted for money, and grants of freedom became common. By the end of the twelfth century there were whole provinces, such as Normandy, in which there was not a single serf.

The lords might not have been so willing to make these adjustments if they had not found it to their advantage to change the old type of agricultural organization. As trade increased, more luxuries came on the market, luxuries which could be acquired only by cash payments. The old rents (mostly payments in kind) and labor services did not produce cash; it was clearly advantageous to commute them for money payments, even if it meant reducing their nominal value. Moreover, the fact that there was now a market for agricultural produce in the towns made it desirable to specialize in producing such things as wool or wine, and to give up the old subsistence economy. The easiest way to do this was for the lord to rent his lands to a man producing for the market; but if he did this, then he had no great need for the labor services of his peasants. The Cistercian monks, who were forbidden to have serfs, were pioneers in this development; they used much of their land for sheep-raising and became the greatest wool-growers of Europe.

It is easy to exaggerate the extent of these changes. Europe remained largely agricultural in spite of the growth of towns; many agricultural villages were still isolated and relatively self-sufficient; serfdom continued to exist in many places and even the free peasants did not have a very high standard of living. But after making these reservations it is still true that there had been a profound change in economic activity. A growing network of trade-routes was binding Western Europe into a single economic unit. Some of the elementary principles of division of labor and specialization had been discovered and this increased production and improved quality. Greater mobility of the population gave more opportunities to the individual and supplied the manpower for new activities. For the first time since the great days of Mediterranean civilization there was a surplus of labor and a surplus of food which made it possible to take chances, to try new techniques, to develop new interests. The economic revival gave a material basis for the optimism and energy which had been stimulated by the political and religious revivals.

3

The Flowering
of
Medieval
Civilization

WILLIAM THE CONQUEROR'S CHURCH OF ST. ÉTIENNE AT CAEN

I. THE TEMPER OF THE TWELFTH CENTURY

WESTERN EUROPE, in the last years of the eleventh century, had made remarkable advances in social organization, in intellectual interests, and in the intangible qualities of spirit and conscience which make civilization possible. This improvement continued at an accelerated rate during the twelfth century. The people of Western Europe showed tremendous energy and persistence in all their activities—religious, political, economic, and cultural. They had a willingness to experiment with new types of organization, a receptiveness to new ideas, an originality in solving their problems which has seldom been equaled. They produced remarkable leaders who gave form and substance to their aspirations and ideals, but the leaders would have had little success if they had not been supported by the efforts and desires of thousands of anonymous workers. Great churchmen, like St. Bernard, were almost entirely dependent on public opinion; they could dominate Europe because the people of Europe believed in the ideals which they expressed. Great kings, like Henry II of England, drew their strength from the general desire for law and order. Abelard was a great teacher because he had eager students; he could hardly live without an audience. Abbot Suger of St. Denis could build the first Gothic church only because hundreds of experiments in new architectural devices had been made in the churches of France. It is hardly necessary to point out that the building of new towns, the establishment of new businesses, and the clearing of new land needed group efforts as well as the initiative of a few wealthy entrepreneurs.

But if the civilization of the twelfth century was the work of a large part of the Western European population, then it is important to know what were the dominant interests and ideals of this population. This is a difficult problem in any period, and is especially difficult for a century in which many classes left no written record of their beliefs. We shall have to reason from effect to cause; we shall have to deduce political, religious, and economic beliefs from literary and artistic monuments. Both procedures are dangerous if pushed too far, and we must be content with a broad outline in which some of the detail must remain obscure.

In the first place, it is clear that the dominant ideals were those inspired by the Christian faith as interpreted by the Church. Not everyone lived up to these ideals, but everyone was affected by them. Kings and great lords might defy the Church for a few years, but they could seldom hold out indefinitely. Ordinary men might sin, but they were careful to do penance before their situation became dangerous. More important than the coercive power of the Church was the spirit of voluntary co-operation which it aroused. The twelfth century was a great century for gifts to the Church; the rich gave lands and money while the poor contributed their labor. It was also a great century for monasteries. The old Benedictine houses grew slowly, but the new and more severe orders such as the Cistercians could hardly find room for their recruits. Moreover, almost all secular activity was placed under religious patronage. It was almost unthinkable to build a bridge or a castle without adding a chapel. Each occupation had its patron saints, its festivals, and its religious processions. Religion dominated the climate of opinion so that even the selfish (who were numerous) and the skeptics (who were rare) expressed their thoughts in terms of orthodox piety.

But the religion of the twelfth century was not quite the same as the religion of earlier periods. If human life was becoming more Christian, Christianity in the West was becoming more human. There was more emphasis on the human side of the Christian story, on the Nativity and the infancy of Jesus, on the Virgin as the human intercessor with the Divine Judge. Underneath conventional expressions of pessimism the men of the twelfth century hid a great deal of optimism; they could not believe that very many of their own people were going to be damned. Human beings were frail, but Jesus had been a helpless child and the Virgin a suffering mother; they could understand and have compassion on human weakness. Therefore the thousands of churches dedicated to the Virgin, the countless statues and reliefs of the Mother and Child, the stories of the Miracles of Our Lady—all emphasizing divine love and forgiveness. Yet the optimism of the twelfth century, while genuine, was not self-deluding. Human efforts were not enough to assure salvation, but the effort had to be made to justify divine intervention. There was a strong desire for more intense and more personal religious experience, and a demand that secular and religious leaders set examples of moral living. The twelfth century was a great century for monasticism because so many men felt that they could gain the intense religious experience which they desired only under the rigors of monastic life. But it was a great century for mystics also, because even the monastery could not satisfy the desire of some men for intense, inner religious experience. Long meditation on the mysteries of the Incarnation and the love of God for man brought flashes of illumination in which the soul seemed very close to the ultimate verities. And for the vast majority who could be neither monks nor mystics there were at least opportunities to hear and see the great saints and preachers. Allowing for all exaggeration, it is still evident that a great religious leader like St. Bernard could attract and influence crowds of almost unbelievable size.

The second important group of ideals centered around the concept of justice. There was obviously strong religious influence here; justice was one of the virtues emphasized by the Church, and the divine law was supposed to underlie all human legislation. This Christian tradition of justice was reinforced by the realities of twelfth-century politics. The chief, and in many cases the only, function of government was the administration of justice. The power of rulers depended largely on the reputation of their courts. The most effective way to punish a strong vassal was to persuade his fellow-vassals that he had been justly condemned in court; then the feudal army would rally behind the lord. Justice, to a twelfth-century man, was the key to good government, peace, and security.

For this reason, the men of the twelfth century made a tremendous effort to improve their judicial systems. In the South the study of Roman law was revived; in the North the customary laws were worked over until a start at their codification could be made. An authoritative summary of the law of the Church (canon law) was given in the *Decretum* of the monk Gratian. At the same time that the law was being restated in a more logical and consistent way, there was a wide-spread attempt to improve procedure. Early medieval courts had been almost helpless when faced with contradictory statements by opposing parties; they took refuge in the judgment of God. During the twelfth century, there was general dissatisfaction with the old methods of compurgation and ordeal, and many experiments with new methods of proof were devised. In regions of customary law an attempt was made to get at the facts through questioning of witnesses or the use of juries. In regions where the Roman law tradition was strong, the judge was given power to decide a case after an examination of oral and written testimony. Everywhere there was an attempt to secure solid evidence, in one way or another, and to base decisions on evidence.

Even more important than these technical improvements was a change in the spirit of the people, a growing desire to obtain legal solutions of controversies instead of fighting them out. In fact, this pressure from below was at least as influential in bringing about changes in administration of justice as planning from above. When more people sought the courts, the courts had to become more efficient. When courts tried many cases a month instead of two or three a year, they gained the experience which made it possible to develop a more rational jurisprudence. This desire to obtain a peaceful solution to controversies had even wider consequences. Whereas the first half of the twelfth century saw serious disorders in all the countries of Western Europe, in the second half there was more willingness to accept the rule of constituted authorities. Henry II of England and Frederick Barbarossa of Germany were both able men, but it was not merely their force of character which calmed their countries after a generation of civil war; it was the general desire for peace. In fact, both Henry and Frederick reached the throne as a result of a compromise between warring parties; even the feudal aristocracy was tired of fighting. Even more striking is the case of Louis VII of France, a king whom no one has ever considered especially able. Yet this respectable mediocrity was more widely obeyed and had more influence in France than any of his predecessors; it was in his reign that great vassals first began to accept decisions of his court.

The Christian faith and the ideal of justice affected almost everyone in Western Europe. Less widespread than these was the desire for knowledge, and yet it influenced thousands of men (and even a few women) of all classes. Here again there are obvious connections among the movements. Some of the interest in religion was bound to take the form of theological studies; some of the interest in justice was bound to lead to a revival of legal studies. But the desire for knowledge had roots of its own; there was a love of study for its own sake, independent of its utility for Church or government. Conservatives were worried about this independence. St. Bernard was offended by the way in which advanced theologians tried to define the mysteries of ardent faith with cold reason, and some rulers had an almost equal dislike for the rationalism of Roman law. But the love of learning was strong enough to overcome all opposition. The students of the twelfth century seized on every bit of knowledge with almost indiscriminate avidity. They read the Latin classics; they analyzed the texts of Roman law; they read and commented on the works of the Fathers of the Church. Even this did not satisfy them. The most adventurous scholars knew that the Moslems had great stores of knowledge and they went down into Moorish Spain to tap these new sources of information. Others worked in Sicily, where there were still Arab and Greek scholars; still others went to Constantinople to obtain translations of Greek texts. The work was difficult, for there were no grammars and dictionaries of the Eastern languages, and the first translations from Arabic and Greek were clumsy and inaccurate. But these struggling scholars accomplished a great work; they renewed Western knowledge of Greek science and philosophy and added the treasures of Arabic mathematics and medicine. Western Europe had never had this material before. The Late Empire had almost abandoned the study of Greek, and Carolingian scholars had been fully occupied in saving the Latin and Christian classics. With all its defects of dogmatism and *a priori* reasoning, with all its contamination by astrology and magic, Graeco-Arabic science still had a stimulating effect on Western thought. It started men thinking about basic scientific problems, and the translations of the twelfth century started a line of investigation which led in the end to Copernicus and Galileo.

We shall never know the number of students who attended the lectures of the great teachers of the twelfth century, but it was large enough to have important effects on European society. The old monastic schools could not absorb the flood of students. They began to congregate in cities where many masters could teach simultaneously, and by the end of the century the larger city schools had become universities. The long-run importance of universities is obvious; even in their infancy they began to influence European life. There were now thousands of educated men, trained in the rational solution of difficult problems, in oral and written expressions of their ideas, in logical organization of scattered materials. These were exactly the qualities for which bishops and counts, popes and kings were searching. University-trained men began to enter the administrative services of the Church and the Western kingdoms. By the end of the century they had a majority of the high positions in the Church and a strong foothold in secular governments. They had much to do with the improvements in the administration of justice which have already been mentioned, and they founded the first bureaucracies in the states of Western Europe. Because they held key positions, their influence was great. Rationalism and legalism were their guiding principles, and by the end of the century Western Europe was thoroughly imbued with these ideas.

Most difficult to discuss of all the ideals of the twelfth century are those associated with its economic activities. The other ideals are open—these are concealed; the others are discussed at length in contemporary literature—these are mentioned only in passing. Certainly many men in the twelfth century were ambitious. They wanted to better themselves, to rise in the world, to attain power and fortune. They had plenty of examples to encourage them, for the twelfth century was a period of opportunity, when a boy who begged his way through the schools of Paris could become pope, and the fourth son of a minor vassal could become earl of Pembroke and Regent of England. Certainly many men in the twelfth century who were already well off wanted more money, in order to live more comfortably and enjoy the new luxuries which were just becoming available. The lords who rented their domain lands to the highest bidder, the merchants who took the moral and physical risks of trading with the infidel, were surely seeking profits.

Yet it would be a mistake to assume that the profit motive was as strong in the twelfth century as it is today. The largest group of ambitious men, those from the peasant class, were seeking improved status rather than greater wealth. The peasant who went to the German frontier to clear new land, or to a Flemish town to work in the textile industry, did not necessarily increase his income. What he gained was more freedom for himself and greater opportunities for his children. The students, as a group, also gained more in status than in money. Most of them did become members of the clergy, which was a step up in the world, but the number of really profitable positions in the Church was far smaller than the number of students available to fill them. The men who worked on translations from the Arabic seldom gained high office, and students of the classics were not much better off. The study of law was a surer road to preferment, and certainly many law students were seeking profit and power rather than pure knowledge. Yet even among the lawyers there were men who were interested in jurisprudence for its own sake. As for the feudal nobility, while they were always eager to obtain new estates through marriage alliances or the favor of their lords, they certainly did not think of their lands primarily as investments. Lordship was still more important than landlordship. The prestige which came from commanding a large group of subordinates was at least as desirable as the money which the subordinates gave to their superiors. And although the landholding class did make an effort to increase income by renting domain lands or encouraging peasants to clear forests and wastes, they had a tendency to spend the money as fast as it came in. Feudal lords were not good businessmen, and would not have considered it a compliment if they had been called so. "Largesse"—free and easy spending—was their ideal, not thrift. They wanted to "live nobly," in a manner befitting their status; they wanted to have a reputation for generosity and open-handed hospitality. They were more apt to run into hopeless debt than to make shrewd investments which would increase their income.

This leaves the bourgeoisie, the class of merchants and master artisans, as the one group which might be expected to be dominated by the profit motive. Certainly it was strong with them, for they could obtain the necessities of life only with the money which came from profitable business transactions. Status meant less to them than to other groups, and money more, and because they prized money they were more skilled in using it to increase their wealth. They knew how to split the risks of a long voyage by selling shares in a ship; they were learning about loans and interest. Money-changers were able to profit through their knowledge of rates of exchange, and great merchants gave and received credit in many transactions. As Pirenne, the famous Belgian historian, claimed, some of the practices and much of the spirit of modern capitalism were already apparent in the twelfth century.

But even in the towns the profit motive was not entirely dominant. External restraints were not important; the guilds had not yet developed detailed regulations and the Church was much less worried about loans at interest and excessive profits than it was to be in the next century. The restraints were rather those which were inherent in the nature of early medieval business. Merchants and artisans were still a small minority in a society which did not especially admire or honor them; they had to give each other mutual support in order to preserve their rights and property. Merchants were safe only if they traveled in companies under semi-military organization. Towns could gain and keep self-government only if all the inhabitants of a town worked together for their common ends. Sharing common dangers meant that business opportunities also had to be shared. All the merchants in a caravan had to be given an equal opportunity to sell their goods in a foreign market; all the retailers in a town had to be given an equal opportunity to buy from foreign wholesalers. Great concentrations of wealth were therefore rare, and few individuals had great economic power.

To sum up, while ambition and the desire for worldly success were common in the twelfth century, they were not always associated with the desire to make money. Improvement in status was the most common ambition; wealth was less important than such things as personal freedom, titles, high office, or the reputation of a scholar. These objectives could often be obtained without economic manipulations, through the favor of princes or prelates, or the aid of family and friends. A higher standard of living usually accompanied improvements in status, but this was often a secondary consideration. Even the townsmen, who had to think in terms of money-making in order to survive, were not always able to give priority to individual economic gain: they had to preserve the prosperity of the group to which they belonged. The full power of money had not yet been revealed; the banker and the entrepreneur were comparatively minor figures in the twelfth century.

II. THE COMMONWEALTH OF CHRISTENDOM

In medieval theory the Christian people of the West formed a single community, united in allegiance to the Roman Church, united in opposition to the infidel and schismatic groups that surrounded them on three sides. This theory had been realized, to some extent, in the Carolingian period, but it had been difficult to apply during the troubled years which followed the break-up of the Carolingian Empire. The greater security, the improvement in communications, the better organization of religious and secular governments gave a new opportunity in the twelfth century to turn the theory of Christian unity into fact. If there ever was a Commonwealth of Christendom it existed at this time. Localism had been largely overcome; nationalism was not yet a divisive factor. Men of ability could receive fiefs or obtain high positions in the Church in any region, no matter where they were born. Even peasants migrated freely across local and national frontiers —witness the thousands of Flemings who settled on the eastern border of Germany. The leadership of the Church was universally acknowledged, and the Church set standards and established objectives for all the West. It had a common internal policy of peace and justice, and a common foreign policy of defense of the Holy Places against the Moslems. During the twelfth century the Church was reasonably successful in gaining the support of the people of Western Europe for these policies.

The Church had great advantages in seeking to maintain and extend its leadership. It was the only really universal institution in Europe. The Empire, which claimed theoretical universality, actually included only Germany, part of Italy, and the old middle kingdom. Moreover the Empire, greatly weakened by the struggle between Henry IV and the Church, had little prestige during the first part of the century. The Church had more than its share of administrative experts and intellectual leaders, thanks to the fact that it offered opportunities to men of the middle and lower classes. Not that the Church ignored status altogether—most bishops and abbots were well born—but it did promote men who would have had little chance of recognition by secular rulers. Finally, while government was improving everywhere, the government of the Church made greater advances during the century than that of any other organization. The administrative control of the pope over the bishops was increased; the judicial system was improved; records were better kept and revenues more efficiently collected. Not until the thirteenth century did any secular state reach the high level of organization which the Church attained in the twelfth.

This ecclesiastical government, developing slowly through several generations, was naturally more effective in the last half of the twelfth century. In the first half, leadership was exercised more by local bishops and abbots than by the pope and his court. Such men were to be found in every part of Europe, carrying on the great work of reform which had begun in the preceding century, directing and stimulating the new piety, advising rulers, and at times even governing kingdoms. Of these leaders, by far the ablest was St. Bernard, who was, for a generation, the uncrowned ruler of the Commonwealth of Christendom.

St. Bernard was born of a noble family in Burgundy in 1093.

He entered the recently founded monastery of Cîteaux at the age of twenty-one, where his unusual ability was quickly recognized. Soon he was sent to found a new house of the Order at Clairvaux, and he remained abbot of Clairvaux, refusing all promotion, until his death.

Clairvaux, under St. Bernard, was a model monastery, famous for the asceticism and spiritual intensity of its life. Yet there were other abbots who enforced their rules as strictly, who mortified the flesh as severely, who never had anything like the influence of St. Bernard. He was not only the ideal monk; he was a great orator and writer, who incarnated the religious ideals and aspirations of his time. He was almost irresistible when he preached to crowds or conferred with kings and princes. His letters were nearly as powerful—clear and logical, yet ablaze with passionate conviction. As Dante saw, the central idea in St. Bernard's thought is love—the undeserved love of God for man, the frail and insufficient love of man for God—and it was because his contemporaries felt the power of this love that they were influenced by St. Bernard. Few men have ever written about their religious beliefs with so much sincerity and frankness—modern readers are almost embarrassed by these revelations of deep feelings. There was an unsympathetic side to St. Bernard—his utter certainty that he was right, his angry denunciations of those who opposed him— but this probably bothers us more than it did his contemporaries. After all, he was a saint, as everyone knew at the time, and saints have always been permitted to be a little emphatic. Moreover, St. Bernard was not vindictive. He could preach against heretics without demanding their death; he could secure the condemnation of Abelard's theological teachings without interfering with Abelard's comfortable retirement in the monastery of Cluny.

As a spiritual leader St. Bernard gave form and direction to all the religious interests of the twelfth century. He gave his own Order such prestige that hundreds of new Cistercian monasteries were founded in every part of Europe. He worked steadily for the independence of the Church and denounced any ruler who tried to place unworthy men in episcopal office. He was an ardent supporter of the cult of the Virgin; his hymns and sermons expressed the deepest yearnings of popular piety. As a conservative theologian, he considered faith far more important than reason, and fought the rationalistic tendencies of some contemporary teachers. He was one of the great mystics of the Church, one of the chief sources from whom later mystics drew their inspiration.

St. Bernard always said, quite sincerely, that he was happy only in his narrow cell at Clairvaux. Yet his sense of duty was so strong that again and again he was forced to leave his monastery in order to carry through programs which he felt were essential to the welfare of the Church. For example, he could not rest until he had settled the contested papal election of 1130. This was the first dispute since the creation of the College of Cardinals in 1059 in which there could be real doubt about the merits of the case. The cardinals had not been unanimous in their choice, but a majority had voted for Anaclete II. St. Bernard never felt bound by mere majorities; he believed that the other candidate, Innocent II, was a better man and had the support of the better element in the Church. He worked strenuously to convince the governments of Europe that he was right, and after years of argument gained the support of the king of France, the emperor of Germany, the chief opponent of the emperor, the cities of north Italy, and finally of Rome. The recognition of Innocent II as pope gave St. Bernard increasing influence in the central government of the Church. During the last years of St. Bernard's life the pope was a former monk of Clairvaux, very responsive to the suggestions of his old abbot.

Another example of St. Bernard's influence was the Second Crusade. He had always been interested in the Christian colony in the Levant; he had helped in drafting the Rule for the Order of the Temple which organized that famous group of knights under semi-monastic vows for the protection of Jerusalem. In 1144 the Moslems conquered the county of Edessa, a Christian outpost which protected the left flank of the Crusading kingdom. St. Bernard immediately began to preach a Crusade. After stirring up great enthusiasm in France, where the king took the cross, he moved to Germany, where he had almost equal success. When the emperor, Conrad III, finally yielded to St. Bernard's arguments, he remarked that only a saint with miraculous powers could have persuaded him to become a Crusader. Unfortunately, that was the only miracle in favor of the expedition. The Crusade was badly led and accomplished nothing; its failure certainly saddened St. Bernard and may have contributed to his death in 1153.

While the saints were stimulating and guiding popular piety, the administrators and lawyers were perfecting the organization of the Church. Their work was absolutely essential if the Church was to keep its independence and make good its claims to leadership. If laymen were to be kept from interfering with the choice of ecclesiastical officials, then the Church had to perfect its own techniques of selection and supervision. A disputed election of a bishop, for example, was a standing invitation to lay interference. The pope had to intervene promptly and decisively in such cases, give a decision based on available evidence, and enforce it with all his authority. Again, in the highly religious twelfth century, it was dangerous to allow clergymen to continue in office who were openly immoral or who used their positions to build up their own private power. Such clerics practically invited laymen to rebel against their authority; some machinery had to be devised by which they could be removed by their ecclesiastical superiors. Thus a whole jurisprudence had to be developed concerning election to and removal from office in the Church. Since all important cases went to the pope, either directly, or on appeal, the end result was to increase greatly his administrative authority. It soon became obvious that the easiest way to avoid trouble was for the pope to make all important appointments himself, rather than to rely on the doubtful chance of unanimous elections by the local clergy. More and more legal excuses were found for this policy and by the end of the century papal appointment of bishops was common, especially in Italy. Elsewhere the papacy had to make compromises with local authorities, but by 1200 no one could become a bishop without papal approval and many bishops owed their office solely to papal nomination.

For much the same reasons the jurisdiction of the clergy over laymen was strengthened and centralized. The Church had always had control of family relationships—marriage, annulments of marriage, questions of legitimacy, and inheritance of personal property, though not of fiefs. This control could easily have important political implications in a feudal society—the annulment of a marriage could tear a great French province from the hands of the Capetian kings and throw it into those of their rivals of England. This was obviously another place where exact procedure and centralized control were necessary. A strong ruler might bully local bishops into recognizing an illegal marriage or annulling a valid one; it was almost impossible to put such pressure on the Roman court and on the pope. In the same way the power to excommunicate unrepentant sinners needed to be carefully supervised. Many men were excommunicated for disobedience to ecclesiastical authorities; it was important to be sure that the excommunication was justified, and, if it was, that it be enforced without fear of secular rulers.

The solution for all these problems was the creation of an elaborate system of ecclesiastical justice. Local courts were carefully organized and staffed with trained lawyers; appeals ran from them to the pope and his legal advisers. The Church secured greater uniformity in and more respect for its law by this method. On the other hand, it became deeply involved in administrative and legal routine. The age of the great monastic leaders was succeeded by the age of the great lawyers. By the last quarter of the century the surest road to advancement in the Church was to study canon law. From Alexander III (1159–1181) through Boniface VIII (1294–1303) the strongest popes were trained in law, and their example naturally influenced the rest of the hierarchy. This trend made the Church more efficient as a government; its greatest political victories were scored under the leadership of the lawyer-popes. But concentration on administration gradually weakened the spiritual leadership of the Church, which was the real source of its strength.

St. Bernard, who saw the change beginning, denounced it with his usual vigor, and his warnings were repeated by many other thoughtful men. Yet it is hard to see how the danger could have been avoided. If the Church was to remain independent of lay authority—and St. Bernard wanted this as much as anyone—it had to develop a strong central administration. Once the administration had developed it had to be run by men who understood it and who knew how to make it work. Dean Inge said once that in religion nothing fails like success and the history of most religious groups—of most mass organizations, for that matter—supports his statement. If basic principles are to be preserved, central organization is necessary, but this always brings to the front men who are more interested in the organization than in the principles. But the danger, though apparent even in the twelfth century, did not seriously harm the Church in that period. It strengthened its leadership of Western society and secured support for its policies until well into the next century.

III. THE DEVELOPMENT OF SECULAR GOVERNMENTS

Within the Commonwealth of Christendom were kingdoms, principalities, and semi-independent towns in various stages of political development. None of these political units was based on nationalism, though some of them had boundaries which coincided roughly with those of modern nations. None of them was a sovereign state, in our sense of the word; that is, nowhere could one find a government completely independent of external authority and completely supreme over all its subordinates. Every ruler recognized the authority of the Church; most rulers (including many kings) were at least nominally vassals of some higher lord. Monarchs who were free from all bonds of vassalage, such as the king of France, were yet not in complete control of their own realms. It is not surprising that the king of France had nothing to say about the government of Normandy; after all, that fief was held by the immensely powerful king of England. But the king of France had little more authority in the petty counties along his northeastern frontier, or in the autonomous bishoprics of south France. Everywhere there was an overlapping of rights of government; the same individuals might be subject to many authorities. The Church could judge cases of legitimacy, and the king cases of failure to give feudal service; murder might be tried in the court of a duke or a count, and petty larceny would be the affair of the local lord or town. These arrangements were confusing, even to men of the twelfth century, who accepted them as natural and inevitable. They were endurable only because no government asked very much of its subjects and therefore seldom came into conflict with other authorities.

But these conditions could not continue indefinitely. As we have seen, justice was one of the dominant ideals of the twelfth century, which meant that governments had to be more actively concerned with it. The more active governments were, the more chance there was for conflicts of authority, and justice could hardly be secured in a state where no one had final responsibility. Therefore the twelfth century saw a clarification of lines of authority. Some governments were weakened until they had no real power; others gained freedom from superior and effective control over inferior jurisdictions. This great sorting out of political powers was not completed in the twelfth century, but some of the most important results were already foreshadowed by 1200. In some parts of Europe, such as Germany and Italy, local government was growing at the expense of central government. In other areas, such as England and France, royal government was becoming stronger and local authorities were beginning to lose their independence.

Germany and Italy were, of course, nominally united under the rule of the emperor. Actually the Empire had been so badly shaken by the struggle with Gregory VII and his successors that it had little vitality during the first half of the century. Henry V had managed to restore peace by deferring to the great nobles and by giving up some of his control over the appointment of bishops in the Concordat of Worms, an agreement made with the pope in 1122. But his death in 1125 without a male heir added a new complication. Two families, the Hohenstaufen and the Welfs (or Guelfs), claimed the throne, and for the next generation Germany was almost evenly divided between their supporters. There were several civil wars, and even in periods of peace the emperor had little authority. Finally, in 1152, the Hohenstaufen Frederick I (called Barbarossa because of his red beard) came to the throne. His mother had been a Welf, which helped conciliate the opposition, and he himself was one of the ablest rulers of the Middle Ages. He was better obeyed than any of his immediate predecessors, and during his long reign (1152–1190) he had a real opportunity to unite Germany and to restore the prestige of the Empire.

He came very near to success in both objectives, but the double task was probably beyond anyone's power. Germany alone was bad enough. The emperor had little land, a small income, and almost no administrative organization to help him govern, whereas the Welfs held the two great duchies of Bavaria and Saxony. Other lords were nearly as strong, and a group of tough new principalities was growing up on the eastern frontier, where the Slavs were in full retreat. The clergy could not be relied on entirely, and since many of the bishops were great territorial lords, this was a serious weakness. Frederick did have in his favor that desire for peace and justice which was so strong everywhere in twelfth-century Europe, but it took great ability to turn it to his advantage in a country where local lords had so much power and prestige. Perhaps he learned some tricks of the trade from his fellow monarchs of France and England; certainly he used what resources he had with skill and determination. His own inheritance was the duchy of Swabia, the hilly, wooded southwest corner of Germany. Here he tried to create a royal domain, something like that of the French king in the Île de France, in which his authority would be unquestioned and from which he could draw a sure income. Monasteries and towns under his protection were induced to give him regular payments. This system was apparently advantageous to both parties, for it spread beyond Swabia into other parts of west Germany.

While creating a solid core of strength in Swabia, Frederick tried to strengthen his authority in the rest of the country by building up feudal relationships between himself and the greater lords. As we saw earlier, feudalism came late to Germany and never included all noble lands or noble men. The kings of England and France had found that feudal lordship gave them their best excuse for controlling their most powerful subjects, and Frederick seems to have felt that his power would be increased if all the great men were his vassals. His policy passed a successful test late in the reign when he had a serious quarrel with Henry the Lion, the Welf duke of Bavaria and Saxony. Frederick received such general support in Germany that he was able to condemn Henry in his court and confiscate his duchies, with a minimum of fighting. But his triumph was not quite complete because the German feudal system was not quite complete. Henry retained extensive lands around Brunswick, which were not held of the king, and his heirs were able to use this territory as a basis for new revolts in the thirteenth century. Frederick did not feel strong enough to keep the confiscated duchies in this own hand; the best he could do was to divide them among some of his supporters.

While Frederick was making important progress in Germany, he did not neglect the Empire. He tried to assert imperial authority in the kingdom of Burgundy, a fragment of the old middle kingdom which lay between the Rhône and the Alps and was almost entirely French-speaking. Here he made some gains by relying on his recently successful device of strengthening and multiplying feudal bonds. But his real effort was reserved for Italy, where he spent at least a fourth of his reign. He had all the old reasons for intervention in Italy, since he believed wholeheartedly in the value of the Empire, and it could not be a going concern without possession of north Italy and some kind of arrangement with the papacy. But to the old reasons was added a new one—the wealth of the Italian cities. Frederick was already drawing a large income from German towns; he must have wondered how much more would be produced by the richer towns of the Lombard plain. If a royal domain in Swabia were valuable, how much more valuable would be a domain in Lombardy.

There were no great dukes in Italy, as there were in Germany, to thwart Frederick's plans, and for a while everything went well for him. The rights of the Empire were acknowledged by everyone, and the pope was not at first unfriendly, since he needed Frederick's help to put down a revolution in his own city of Rome. But as Frederick persisted in his Italian intervention he created a strong opposition to his plans. Alexander III, who became pope in 1159, had definite ideas about the inferiority of the Empire to the Church and was worried by Frederick's growing power. The towns of Lombardy, whose quarrels with each other had facilitated Frederick's advance, became frightened enough to forget their rivalries and unite against the emperor. Under papal patronage a Lombard League was formed—a union of north Italian towns to preserve their autonomy.

Frederick was at first scornful of his opponents. He tried to check the pope by supporting a series of anti-popes, and he felt sure that his well-trained German troops could defeat any city militia. But the Italian towns were not like those of the North; the nobility lived in them rather than in the open country and their magistrates and captains were men with as much military experience as any German knight. Frederick was completely defeated by the Lombard League at Legnano in 1176, and his dream of direct rule over north Italy vanished with that battle.

Frederick's remarkable political ability was never better shown than after this defeat. He cut his losses by a quick reconciliation with the pope and so was able to make a fairly reasonable agreement with the Lombard League at Constance in 1183. Although the towns gained complete autonomy, they recognized the lordship of the emperor and agreed to give him annual payments in return for their rights of self-government. Meanwhile he shifted his base to the south. The towns of Tuscany were less advanced than those of Lombardy, and Frederick was able to gain a strong position in that area without much trouble. Then he accomplished the remarkable feat of marrying his eldest son to the heiress of the Norman kingdom of Sicily, a state which had long been a supporter of the papacy and an opponent of the Empire. This was Frederick's last great success; he died soon after as a participant in the Third Crusade.

Frederick had accomplished a great deal in both Germany and Italy, but he had not quite succeeded in making a real state out of either Germany or the Empire. Permanent institutions of government, which could operate even when the ruler was absent or incompetent, had not been established. Frederick's most useful officials came largely from a class which had once been servile—the *ministeriales* who managed estates, ran minor courts, and were considered far beneath the old nobility. In order to weaken the Welfs he had had to strengthen other families, such as the Wittelsbach, who received Bavaria after the fall of Henry the Lion and kept it until 1918. In order to have support for his expeditions to Italy, he had had to slow down his plans for strengthening central government in Germany. If his heir had had his ability, or even as long a life, these deficiencies might have been repaired. As it was, Henry VI ruled only a few years (1190–1197) and spent most of his time trying to gain control of central and southern Italy. His wife had inherited Sicily, but the Normans of the South were not eager to have a German ruler, even if he were married to one of their princesses. They revolted and maintained their independence for four years. Henry could not attack Sicily without first occupying central Italy, an act which irritated the papacy and many of the towns of the region. The Germans were not particularly interested in Henry's Italian adventure, and their loyalty to the Hohenstaufen dynasty began to weaken.

As a result, when Henry died suddenly in 1197, the whole structure which Frederick Barbarossa had carefully erected fell to pieces. The rights of Henry's heir, the two-year-old Frederick II, were generally ignored. Civil war began in Sicily, and German troops and governors were driven out of Tuscany and central Italy. Civil war also plagued Germany, where the Hohenstaufen Philip, younger brother of Henry VI, and the Welf Otto of Brunswick, heir of Henry the Lion, were competing for the kingship. By the beginning of the thirteenth century there was no effective central government anywhere in the Empire. In Italy the towns became completely independent; in Germany all real authority fell into the hands of the ecclesiastical and secular princes. This trend was never to be reversed. In spite of all efforts to restore the Empire, Italy remained a land of independent city-states and Germany a land of independent principalities for the rest of the Middle Ages.

England marked the other end of the political scale. It was already more united than any other European country at the beginning of the century, thanks to the work of William the Conqueror. William had preserved the Anglo-Saxon system of local government, based on counties administered by sheriffs who were entirely subject to the king. To this he had added a carefully regulated feudalism which kept any one lord from becoming too strong, and subjected all of them to the authority of his court. On this foundation Henry I (1100–1135) and Henry II (1154–1189) were able to raise a structure of central government which was surpassed only by that of the papacy in twelfth-century Europe.

They were able to use to the fullest extent the desire for justice which was so characteristic of the century. Part of the inheritance from the Anglo-Saxon kingdom was the rule that the most important criminal cases were reserved for the king or his agents. The introduction of feudalism by the Conquest added to this jurisdiction over all significant disputes about landed property. Since all great men held their estates of the king, disputes among them could be settled only in the king's court. But these principles were only a starting-point; they did not automatically create the English legal system. At first, criminal cases were tried by sheriffs in county courts using obsolete procedures, while disputes between great men were settled by informal discussion among the chief vassals in the king's presence.

Henry I was a hard and ambitious man, but he did wish to improve the administration of justice in his realm, perhaps because he could see that it would add to his power. The sheriff was the weakest link in the system of royal justice. He was usually chosen because he had military ability and local prestige, not because he was expert in the law. He was occupied with details of administration, the collection of the king's revenue, the defense of his county. He could be a faithful and useful official without being a very good judge. Henry tried various experiments to solve this problem; the most successful was the creation of circuit judges. These men were sent from the king's court to counties where important cases were pending; they superseded the sheriff and gave justice as direct representatives of the king. Since they were chosen among men who had had wide experience at the king's court, they were usually efficient in their work; since they visited many places in the course of their work, they tended to create a more uniform set of legal rules throughout England. Henry sent out circuit judges only when there were difficulties in the local administration of justice, but he used them frequently enough to establish a tradition.

The other great achievement of Henry I was in the field of finance. He wanted to be sure that he received everything due from the wide estates and extensive rights which he had in England. Both the late Anglo-Saxon kings and William the Conqueror had been careful about their revenues. Henry I used precedents from both periods to establish a great central accounting office, the Exchequer. Here the sheriffs, and others who owed the king money, appeared twice a year to render their accounts before a group of the king's closest advisers. The Exchequer knew, from carefully preserved records, exactly what was owed and how much had been paid in. The figures were demonstrated to the often illiterate sheriffs by moving counters about on a table ruled into columns for thousands, hundreds, scores (not tens), and units. This did much to limit usurpation of the royal domain, and ensured a large cash revenue to the king. The importance of both these points should be stressed, since they gave Henry a great advantage over his rivals. Most medieval rulers steadily lost revenue because subordinates quietly annexed property which they were merely supposed to administer. Even when the revenue was collected, it was often paid in kind, which made it less useful. A barnful of grain at the north end of his country was of little help to a king besieging a castle in the south. But Henry kept his income at a high level and received most of it in cash. Thus, though England was very thinly populated—it probably had no more than 1,250,000 inhabitants—Henry was at least as strong as the king of the much larger country of France.

Henry died without male heirs in 1135 and a disputed succession between his daughter and his nephew made the next nineteen years rather barren in the development of English government. The dispute finally ended when both factions, weary of war, agreed to recognize Henry's grandson, Henry II, as king in 1154. Young

Henry promptly resumed the work of strengthening the kingship, and by the time of his death in 1189 the main institutions of the medieval English government were clearly established.

Henry had tremendous energy, real interest in problems of government, and a willingness to experiment with new ideas and institutions. He was also ambitious, greedy, and bad-tempered; he had to have a good government to balance the defects in his character and retain the loyalty of his subjects. He needed an efficient government in England because he could spend little time in that country. More than two-thirds of his reign was passed in France, where he held a great group of fiefs which stretched from the Channel to the Pyrenees. He had inherited Normandy from his mother and Anjou from his father; he secured Aquitaine by marrying Eleanor, the heiress of the duchy and the divorced wife of Louis VII of France. This marriage involved him in an endless round of trouble. The French king was naturally jealous of an overpowerful vassal and successful rival; he stirred up rebellions and made war on Henry whenever he could. Aquitaine was the largest French fief—it occupied the whole southwest corner of the country—but it was full of turbulent and disloyal vassals. Henry could hold his French possessions only if he had a peaceful, well-organized England at his back, able to supply him with men and money.

Henry spent the first years of his reign in restoring order in England and destroying the illegal castles which had been built by rebellious lords during the dispute over the succession. Then, in the 1160's, he began the long series of experiments which created the English judicial system and the English common law. He greatly increased the use of circuit judges and gave them new powers and responsibilities. While his grandfather, Henry I, had sent them out only on special occasions, Henry II moved them through the counties year after year and gave them jurisdiction over all local disputes. More than that, they also supervised all details of local administration. They investigated sheriffs and forest officials; they inquired into possible sources of royal revenue; they reorganized and regulated local government. Through the circuit judges, Henry II was in direct contact with all parts of his kingdom, and his subjects were constantly reminded of his power. His orders could be enforced uniformly throughout the realm and the disobedience or rebelliousness of any official or vassal could be easily checked.

At the same time that Henry was increasing the functions of the circuit judges, he was introducing the use of the jury. The idea was an old one—it went back at least to the Carolingian kings—but it had never been extensively used before. The jury was a device for giving a ruler authentic information; Maitland defined it as "a body of neighbors summoned by a public officer to give upon oath a true answer to a question." Frankish kings had used it to determine boundaries of royal estates, and William the Conqueror had obtained a description of all English landholdings—the famous Domesday survey—by the testimony of jurors in every township. The jury had also been used to settle disputes between great landholders; it gave the king the facts and so enabled him to decide the case without suspicion of favoritism. But it had been used only sparingly by earlier kings. Until the time of Henry II no subject had a right to demand a jury, and no general class of lawsuits was regularly settled by jury verdicts.

Henry's great ability as a ruler was most clearly demonstrated by the way in which he made the jury a regular part of English procedure. There were no sweeping enactments, no edicts that after a certain date all cases must be tried by jurors. Instead he tested it in one type of case after another; he offered it to his subjects as a favor, an alternative procedure which they could use if they liked. They did like it; the verdict of neighbors about the facts in a case was an improvement on older methods of proof, even though the neighbors might depend on hearsay and family tradition. By the end of the reign the jury was used to settle almost all disputes about feudal holdings, by far the most important category of civil cases. It had not made as much progress in criminal trials. Here, where life and limb were at stake, people showed more reluctance to accept mere human testimony instead of the judgment of God. But Henry had succeeded in establishing the grand jury—a jury which collected accusations against suspected criminals and presented them to the judges—and Henry took the accusations of his grand jurors very seriously. A man indicted by a grand jury might be punished or exiled, even if he were cleared by the ordeal. The unfairness of this became obvious in the next century and led to the establishment of the criminal trial jury as we have it today.

We think of the jury as a safeguard against tyranny, but the twelfth-century jury effectively increased royal power in England. The jury in civil cases was so well liked that it gave the king a practical monopoly in this area of justice. The baronial courts, which had been strong and active in the first century after the Conquest, gradually withered away, while the royal courts became crowded with cases. This obviously increased the king's power; it also added to his revenue, since few cases were settled without payment of large fees and fines to the king. The increasing volume of business gave the judges valuable experience; by the end of the century they were keeping excellent records and writing clear and logical treatises on English law. These expert judges were the backbone of the English administration; they were the men who kept the government going during Henry's long absences abroad.

The growing use of juries not only built up the English administrative system; it also gave the English people valuable training in the art of self-government. The jury was such an effective device for obtaining information that Henry used it for all kinds of inquiries and investigations. When the circuit judges visited the counties they carried with them a long list of questions which had to be answered by juries. These juries represented every political subdivision of the country, and a man of any standing in his community was sure to be called on repeatedly for jury service. They did not like this, any more than we do, but they did acquire the habit of participating in the work of government. This was especially true of the class of knights, the vassals of the great barons who had formed the core of the feudal army. They were always preferred for jury service, and some juries had to be composed exclusively of knights. As a result, they became more and more interested in local government and more and more useful to the king. This had two important consequences. In the first place, because the king could get a great deal of unpaid service from the knights he was less inclined to hire bureaucrats to attend to the details of local administration. This tradition remained strong. Clear into the nineteenth century England was a country in which there were few bureaucrats and in which the country gentlemen, the heirs of the knights, had a strong tradition of public service. In the second place, the knights who served on the juries of their counties were actually representing those counties in dealing with royal justices. This made it easy to extend the idea of representation to other areas. When the thirteenth-century kings wanted public support for their policies, they called on the counties to send representative knights to Parliament.

The strength of Henry's work was tested during the reign of his son, Richard Lionheart (1189–1199). Richard was a great soldier, but a rather mediocre king. He spent less than a year in England during the ten years that he ruled, and he demanded more money from the kingdom than any of his predecessors. He was so anxious for a fight that on his way to Palestine in the Third Crusade he quarreled with the king of France, the emperor Henry VI, and the ruler of the Byzantine Empire. This made it a little difficult for him to return home when the Crusade failed. He tried to slip through Central Europe in disguise, but was captured by Germans who turned him over to Henry VI. The Crusade had been expensive enough, but Henry demanded a ransom which was even worse. As soon as this had been paid, and Richard had regained his freedom, he became involved in a war with France which lasted until his death. He saved his French territories, but England paid most of the expenses.

No other twelfth-century government could have stood the double strain of an absentee king and constant war, but the English government actually became stronger during Richard's reign. The judicial system was perfected and stabilized; the first complete court records come from this period. Even more important, direct, general taxes were introduced to pay for the Crusade, the ransom, and the French war. Here again, England gained a distinct advantage over rival governments. General taxation was almost unknown in the early Middle Ages; rulers drew the supplies they needed from their own estates, and got the work of government done through services owed by vassals. In an emergency they might ask their vassals for financial aid, and they could squeeze gifts out of towns and monasteries fairly frequently, but they were not supposed to demand general taxes. The medieval ideal of government was that the king should live "of his own," without taking the property of his subjects.

It is true that Richard's first tax was for a holy purpose, the Crusade, and that this helped break down the prejudice against taxation. But the French king also collected a tax to pay for this Crusade, and aroused so much opposition that the attempt was not repeated for almost a century. In England, the government was able to repeat the tax almost immediately, and at a higher rate, in order to obtain money for Richard's ransom. No other secular government was able to take repeated taxes at so early a date and this increased the financial advantage which England had over her rivals.

The process of centralization began later in France than in England and had not progressed as far by the end of the twelfth century. In 1100 the French king was not even master of his own domain around Paris, where petty vassals defied his orders and oppressed his subjects. The great feudal lords were even more independent, and many of them had more highly developed governments than that of their nominal suzerain. The French king had, however, some potential advantages which made it possible for him to overcome the handicap of a late start. He was the ancient ally of the Church; popes who were having difficulties with the emperor instinctively sought refuge in France and quarrels between French rulers and the papacy were rare. The leading churchmen of France usually supported the king in his efforts to extend his authority. He was feudal lord of all the great dukes and counts of France, which gave him a moral advantage not to be despised. If they made war on him, they were attacking their lord and were presumably in the wrong; even Henry II of England did not push his attacks to the limit. If the king made war on his vassals, he was presumably enforcing his rights as suzerain and did not have to hold back. The king could annex the fief of a rebellious vassal, but the vassal could not hope to annex the royal domain. Finally, the royal domain was fertile, and lay across all the great trade-routes of France. It could be made to produce great wealth, and in time of war it gave the king the advantage of interior lines. It contained the great city of Paris, which was already beginning to acquire its reputation as the intellectual and artistic center of Europe.

The first king to begin the work of strengthening the royal government was Louis VI (1108–1137). He was determined to be master in his own domain of the Île de France and fought steadily and patiently against the petty vassals who defied him from their fortified towers. It was a long and thankless task; some men had to be defeated three or four times before they learned their lesson, and new enemies appeared as fast as old ones were vanquished. But Louis' persistence paid off in the end; by his death he was as well obeyed in his own province as the duke of Normandy or the count of Flanders in theirs. He was less successful in reducing his great vassals to obedience. He could not defeat the duke of Normandy, who was also king of England, and though he gained temporary control of Flanders during a disputed succession, his candidate for the countship was soon driven out. His greatest success was the marriage of his eldest son to Eleanor, heiress of the duchy of Aquitaine, but, as we have seen, this was only a temporary gain, since the marriage was eventually dissolved.

Louis VI was aided, in the latter part of his reign, by one of the great twelfth-century abbots, Suger of St. Denis. Suger was a good example of the opportunities which the Church offered men of low birth. His parents were poor peasants, who gave their son to the monastery of St. Denis while he was still a child. He must have been an intelligent boy, for the monks placed him in their school, where he had as a fellow-student the young prince who was later to be King Louis VI. The two boys became life-long friends, and royal favor may have helped Suger to rise in the world. At the same time he gave early proof of his administrative ability in governing outlying possessions of the abbey, and had already served on several important diplomatic missions when he became abbot in 1122. The abbey of St. Denis stood in a peculiarly close relationship to the king of France. It was the guardian of the sacred relics of the Apostle of Gaul, the burial place of the kings, the center of the royal cult which raised the king so high above his vassals. As protector of St. Denis the king carried its ensign, the Oriflamme, when he went to war; as nominal vassal of St. Denis he held the province of the Vexin which protected Paris on the north from the Normans. Any abbot of St. Denis would have influence, and an abbot of Suger's ability was sure to be one of the leading men at court.

Suger was a business man and a diplomat, not a warrior. He encouraged Louis to put down the petty tyrants of the Île de France, since only in that way could the royal domain be made profitable, but he did his best to keep peace between the king and the great vassals. By tactful dealings with St. Bernard and the pope he cemented the alliance between the French monarchy and the papacy, which had been a little shaken by the opposition of Louis' father to the reform movement. But Suger was very busy with the affairs of his own monastery, which were at least as complicated as those of a great corporation today, and he was not the only man whom Louis trusted.

During the next reign, however, Suger's influence was of the greatest importance. Louis VII (1137–1180) was called Louis the Young during his father's lifetime, and to some extent he deserved the title all his life. He was never quite sure of himself, hesitated long over decisions, avoided full commitment whenever possible. Honest, upright, and sensitive, he disliked the rather tough group of warrior-politicians who had helped Louis VI conquer the Île de France and relied more and more on Suger. The climax of Suger's power came during the Second Crusade. He was left in charge of the kingdom while Louis went to the East, and did a brilliant job as Regent. A threatened rebellion was suppressed; all of Louis' demands for money were met, and there was even a balance in the treasury when the king returned. Unfortunately for Louis, Suger died soon after the Crusade, in 1152, and no other royal servant could take his place.

The death of Suger also led directly to the loss of Aquitaine. Eleanor of Aquitaine was not a very good wife for the quiet and retiring Louis. Raised in the gayest court in France, where the new-fangled ideas of chivalry were just becoming popular, she loved pleasure and adventure. Energetic and intelligent, she had a mind and plans of her own; she would not sink her personality in order to make Louis' reign a success. Even her domineering second husband, Henry II of England, could not control her and finally solved the problem by confining her in a castle. Louis VII could not take such a drastic step, but he did have a good excuse for divorce (they were too closely related) and he began to think of it seriously when the queen gave him some reason to doubt her virtue. While he lived, Suger prevented the break, but within a few months of his death the marriage was annulled. Eleanor, as we have seen, took prompt revenge by marrying Henry II.

In later centuries English possession of Aquitaine was to be a threat to France; at the time of the divorce it mattered less. Louis VII had not been able to prevent private war there, and Henry II had little more success. The vassals of the duchy were so unruly that no ruler could draw much profit from it; Richard Lionheart met his death in trying to enforce his right to treasure-trove against a petty lord of the region. Yet the divorce hurt the prestige of the monarchy, and it says much for the work of Louis VI and Suger that the setback was only temporary.

In spite of the loss of Aquitaine, Louis VII was able to strengthen his position elsewhere. Many petty vassals on the edges of the royal domain began to recognize his authority and ask his aid. They submitted their quarrels to his court and permitted him to intervene in their affairs. Even in the distant south, Louis was asked to protect lesser vassals and fiefs held by the Church against over-powerful neighbors. He could not always intervene successfully, but he did make armed expeditions into Burgundy which greatly strengthened his authority. The duke of Burgundy himself and many of the stronger counts of the region were forced to answer for their misdeeds in the royal court. In short, Louis VII increased the moral authority of the monarchy even if he added little to its material possessions. He took seriously his position as supreme judge and protector of the weak, and he was able to persuade others to accept his claims. For the first time the theoretical suzerainty of the king of France over all his vassals began to be a reality.

Louis' successor, Philip II (1180–1223), was the real founder of strong monarchy in France. Called Augustus, because he conquered so much land for the royal domain, he was also the founder of the French administrative system. His victories were won by diplomacy and intrigue rather than by overwhelming military strength, and were consolidated by developing a new type of royal government. Philip was small, thin, and sickly—not an imposing figure physically—and his moral stature was not much greater.

Sly and treacherous, a master of fifth-column tactics, he looks unheroic beside his great rival, Richard Lionheart. Yet Philip was one of the greatest kings France ever had, and he gave his subjects, old and new, more peace and security than they had possessed for generations.

Philip's first task was to weaken the empire which Henry II had created. As long as the English king ruled western France from the Channel to the Pyrenees, no French king could feel safe. Philip was greatly aided by family quarrels among members of the rival dynasty. Henry's bad temper and unwillingness to share authority angered his sons, who were just as egotistic as he. Philip encouraged their ambitions, and made Henry's last years miserable by backing repeated rebellions of his sons. When Richard became king, Philip intrigued with John, Richard's younger brother. When John succeeded Richard, he, in turn, was harassed by the claims of his nephew, Arthur, to a share in the family possessions. This constant pressure not only weakened the English kings; it also shook the loyalty of many of their vassals. Philip promised wealth, titles, and secure possession of their fiefs to anyone who came over to his side, and so gained many secret adherents in Normandy, Anjou, and Poitou.

Soon after 1200, Philip was given an opportunity to strike. John, whose bad character had cost him the full support of many subjects, wronged one of his vassals in the duchy of Aquitaine by eloping with his fiancée. The vassal appealed to Philip for justice, and Philip summoned John to appear before his court. When John defaulted, he was condemned to lose his fiefs. Philip moved promptly to carry out the sentence of the court, while John made only a half-hearted defense. He did not trust his vassals, and when they saw that he would not give them full support, they went over to Philip. By 1205 he was in full possession of Normandy, Anjou, and the northern strip of Aquitaine. The rest of the duchy was saved only because old Queen Eleanor was still alive and could claim some rights in her old inheritance.

By these conquests Philip tripled the size of the royal domain and made himself stronger than any of his vassals. He raised the prestige of the king's court to new heights. If it could condemn and punish John of England, no other feudal lord could safely defy it. As a result, the rest of Philip's reign was fairly peaceful, with one exception. John made a great effort to regain his lost fiefs in 1214, by allying himself with rebellious barons of the northeast and with the emperor of Germany. But Philip defeated John's allies at Bouvines, while John himself was held in check in Poitou by Prince Louis, Philip's heir. The failure of this great coalition to achieve any success convinced the other barons that it was useless to oppose the king. Philip could devote his last years entirely to administrative problems.

His chief administrative difficulty was that France was not a political unit like England, but a loose federation of provinces. Each province had its own law and customs, its own judicial and financial system. When new provinces were added to the royal domain they could not be deprived of their old laws and institutions. That would have been the surest way to encourage rebellion, for the customs of the people were their birthright, and they would fight savagely to retain them. And yet, if each province were left its own form of government, what had the conquest profited the king? How could he be sure of the loyalty, or draw on the resources, of an autonomous principality ruled by local nobles?

Philip solved this problem by allowing the provinces to keep their old laws and institutions, while placing agents sent out from the royal court in positions where they controlled the local governments. The key official in this arrangement was the *bailli*,[1] a well-paid and well-trained man who had full judicial, financial, and military power in his district. The *bailli* usually had had

---

[1] This is the same word as the English "bailiff," but since the bailiff never had very high rank in English government, it would be a mistake to translate the title of the very powerful French official by this word.

extensive experience in government before he was sent to the provinces and was often a member of the minor nobility, though some members of the middle class attained the rank. But the essential requirement was undeviating loyalty to the king. Cruelty or corruption might be pardoned, as long as the *bailli* kept his province firmly united to the royal domain. For this reason Philip chose most of his *baillis* from the regions near Paris; for this reason he moved them frequently from one district to another, so that they would not form local attachments and loyalties. The *bailli* was constantly reminded that he was the king's man, not the representative or the protector of the people of his province.

Philip's system worked well. His new subjects were reasonably happy since they kept their old laws, and the king ran no danger since the old laws were administered by his agents. The *baillis* kept the peace; they collected large revenues for the king; they attached conquered provinces more firmly every year to the crown. The advantages of this type of administration were so great that it was extended or imitated by all Philip's successors. And yet there were two serious weaknesses in Philip's arrangements—weaknesses which could not have been avoided at the time, but which were to cause trouble in centuries to come. In the first place, the fact that each province had its own laws and institutions complicated the work of government and led to endless delay and inefficiency. Second, and far more important, most of the king's subjects had only provincial interests. Their chief concern was to preserve provincial rights; they had little responsibility for the work of the central government. France was united only in her king and his bureaucracy. For any really important work, the king had to rely on agents sent out from Paris; not, as in England, on local notables. This meant that the people of France never had the training in self-government which those of England received; it meant that the key man in French politics was the bureaucrat and not the country gentleman. Clear into the nineteenth century the history of the two countries reflects this fundamental difference.

IV. NEW IDEAS AND THEIR EXPRESSION IN THE TWELFTH CENTURY

The twelfth century was original and energetic; it developed new ideas and was able to give these ideas enduring form. In this respect it was a worthy rival of the Golden Ages of Greece and of Rome, and its influence on the modern world has been fully as great. For this reason, it is the most important century of the Middle Ages for those who wish to understand Western civilization. We are still influenced in our art and our literature, in our educational system and social relationships, by ideas and institutions of the twelfth century.

As we have seen, there was a growing desire for knowledge during the century. There were few students at the beginning of the century; there were thousands at the end. These men were interested in every scrap of knowledge which they could find; they studied all the texts which were available in Western Europe and made long journeys to Spain and Constantinople to secure Arabic and Greek material which interested them. Their energy was sometimes greater than their judgment; they studied inferior works with the same reverence that they gave to masterpieces, and they gave astrology and magic the same respect as astronomy and mathematics. But they supplied Western Europe with the materials, the problems, and the methods which nourished intense intellectual activity for centuries.

The first task was to learn to use language as a precise instrument in thinking. The language had to be Latin, since none of the vernacular tongues were sufficiently developed or standardized to be used for abstract thought. All men who had any claim to be educated knew Latin, though many of them did not know it very well. Hence there was an important revival of the classics during the first half of the twelfth century in order to increase vocabulary and improve style. At the same time, more and more attention was given to the study of logic. This tendency was criticized then, and has been ridiculed since, but it was a necessary step in the history of medieval thought. The study of logic was helpful in developing clear conceptions and accurate reasoning; it was only when the rules of logic had become an unconscious habit of all European thinkers that the teaching of formal logic could be abandoned. Moreover, interest in logic was one of the main forces which drove Europeans to seek knowledge from the Moslems and the Greeks. Aristotle had written the basic books on logic, but only a small part of his works were available in Latin translation at the beginning of the century. The value of logic seemed so great and interest in it was so high that scholars were willing to make endless efforts to recover the missing books. And in seeking Aristotle's logic they found many other things—Graeco-Arabic science and the stimulating commentaries of Moslem scholars.

Better knowledge of Latin and increased understanding of the rules of logic were of great assistance in the revival of law and theology. Legal studies centered in Italy, where the Roman law had never been wholly forgotten and where some elementary legal treatises had been written in the eleventh century. The first famous teacher of Roman law was Irnerius of Bologna, who established a pattern of study which was followed for generations. Justinian's texts were read line by line, difficult words were explained, the general purpose of the passage stated, and its relations to the rest of the law made clear. This careful analysis turned out men who had real knowledge of the law, and a strong desire for accuracy and precision in composing official documents. The study of Roman law was soon supplemented by the study of canon law, the law of the Church. Here the great name is that of the monk Gratian, who, like Irnerius, taught at Bologna. Canon law was based on decrees of Church Councils, the writings of the early Church Fathers, and decisions of the popes. Obviously this scattered material had to be organized and codified if it were to form a complete and consistent system. There had been some earlier attempts to do this, but Gratian's codification, written about 1141, was the first which was reasonably complete and universally accepted. He made canon law systematic, logical, and self-sustaining, and his great book, the *Decretum*, was soon studied with the same care as the corpus of Roman law. Students flocked to Bologna to study the two laws, and we have already seen that the Bolognese-trained lawyers had great influence in Church and State in the second half of the century. They controlled the Church and advised kings and princes; under their influence the society of Western Europe became more orderly and also more legalistic.

If Italy was the center of legal studies, France was the home of theology. Just as the study of law had never completely died out in Italy, so in France there had been, from the time of Charlemagne, a thin but persistent stream of theological writing. Since the reform movement had centered in France, the leaders of the French clergy were better educated and their schools were more advanced than those of other countries. In the first half of the twelfth century there were many able theologians in France. The most famous and in some ways the most important member of this group was Abelard.

Abelard was the eldest son of a minor vassal in Brittany who was infected with the love of learning which was so typical of the period. He gave up his rights to his father's fief so that he could be free to study in the schools of Paris. His first interest was logic, but when he felt that he was master of this subject he began to use his new intellectual techniques on theology. He was a great teacher and a cantankerous personality; the more famous he became the more enemies he acquired. His fellow-teachers resented his outspoken criticism of their work, and leaders of the reform movement were irritated by his attempts to make faith too rational. His treatise on the Trinity angered St. Bernard, who accused him of placing "degrees in the Trinity, modes in the Majesty, and numbers in the Eternity," in other words, of trying to define by reason a mystery of the faith. His *Sic et Non* (*Yes and No*) was

just as bad, for here he accumulated opinions of the Church
Fathers on both sides of deliberately shocking questions, for
example, "that sin is pleasing to God and the contrary." Abelard's
personal life did not increase his popularity. He seduced Héloïse,
the niece of an influential clergyman of Paris, which was bad
enough for a prominent theologian, and then made matters worse
(by medieval standards) by marrying her, thus barring himself
from promotion in the Church. As a result, when he was accused
of heresy by St. Bernard, he had few friends. His actual guilt was
doubtful, for Abelard was no agnostic, but merely an over-clever
young man who had become a little intoxicated with the wine of
the new learning. But many people were suspicious of him; his
book on the Trinity was condemned, and he was forced to give up
teaching. He retired to the monastery of Cluny, where he died
peacefully in 1142.

Abelard's troubles were largely caused by his difficult personality. Other men used methods which were essentially like his, and
even borrowed directly from his work, without losing their reputation for orthodoxy. They tried to build logical structure into
Christian theology; they tried to derive new propositions from accepted articles of the faith; they consulted the Fathers of the
Church and listed their opinions on both sides of controversial
questions. They were less shocking than Abelard because they were
not innovators and because they were careful not to claim too much
for their methods. They admitted that some articles of the faith
were beyond rational analysis and they were careful to find an
orthodox solution to problems in which they had cited conflicting
authorities. The *Sentences* of Peter Lombard are a good example
of this kind of work, and they became a textbook for the next
generation of students.

Medicine was the only scientific or semi-scientific subject which
drew a large number of students. The basic texts were translated
from the Greek, though some use was made of Arabic experience,
especially in diseases of the eyes. There was much good sense in

this old material, but there were also many errors and omissions. Twelfth-century scholars had such great respect for book knowledge that they seldom used their own observations, much less deliberate experiments, to correct the traditional texts.

The same weakness was apparent in the mathematics and natural science of the twelfth century, though here there was a better excuse for mere assimilation of authoritative texts. Few men ventured into these unrewarding fields, and they could do little more than translate and explain the work of the Greek and Moslem masters. There was so much to learn—the new art of algebra and the even newer art of reckoning by Arabic figures, all the observations and theories discovered by generations of astronomers, the work of Euclid in geometry, and the solid, if rudimentary, observations of the Greeks in physics and biology. It was important that men were again interested in these subjects, important that they learned all that the past had to teach them. There could be no original work until the task of assimilation had been completed.

The great increase in the number of students during the twelfth century posed problems for the Church, the teachers, and the students themselves. The Church was worried about the content and implications of the new learning. After all, most of it came from pagan or infidel sources; there was much in Aristotle and even more in his Moslem commentators which seemed to contradict Christian belief. Even if this danger was avoided, the Church feared the excessive rationalism of scholars who thought they could find a logical explanation for everything. St. Bernard was not the only religious leader who was worried, and Abelard was not the only scholar who had to face a heresy trial. The teachers had the problems of collecting fees from wandering, propertyless scholars, and of meeting competition from unqualified charlatans who promised short cuts to learning. The students were almost always strangers in the towns where they congregated, and were regularly overcharged and sometimes maltreated by the townsmen. The little cathedral and monastery schools which already existed could not deal with these problems; the cathedral clergy and the monks had too many other duties to spend much time on reorganizing their educational system. Some new institution was necessary, and during the second half of the twelfth century the university was gradually developed.

The first university was probably at Bologna, the center of legal studies. Law students were mature men, who had already completed the preliminary arts course; they resented being fleeced by the townspeople and even suspected that some of their professors were not giving them their money's worth. They organized to protect their interests and drew up regulations limiting the prices of rooms and food and specifying the minimum content of courses. The professors, in self-defense, formed their own corporation, which set standards for admission to the teaching profession. At Paris, where most students were boys taking the preliminary arts course in language and logic, the professors were the first to organize. They adopted rules to ensure that all teachers were properly qualified. No one could be admitted to higher studies, such as theology, until he had passed the arts course; no one could teach until he had graduated from the appropriate faculty. The Church was especially interested in Paris because it had the strongest theological faculty, and at the end of the century the pope confirmed the corporate status of the university. Thus the basic features of the modern university were already developed by 1200. Students attended regularly organized courses; they prepared for examinations, and if they passed they received a teaching license, or, as we would say, a degree. All this seems so natural that it is hard to imagine any other arrangement, and yet it marked a great change from earlier, more individualistic methods of instruction.

The scholars of the twelfth century influenced their own age directly by encouraging more rational and orderly organization of social activity. As we have seen, they played an important part in the improvement of ecclesiastical and secular government.

Better knowledge of law facilitated the growth of large-scale business, since contracts and agreements could be drafted more precisely. University organization made possible the steady development of learning, and the translations from Greek and Arabic scientific treatises laid the foundation for later original work. But, like most scholars, those of the twelfth century seldom wrote well; few people read their books or are influenced by their ideas today. The most direct influence of the twelfth century on our own thinking comes from men who were not primarily scholars, and who wrote for a wider audience than that of the university-trained reader.

First among these influential writers would come the religious leaders, even though they wrote in Latin. Twelfth-century Latin was more like the vernacular, both in vocabulary and syntax, than that of the classical period; it was understood by many laymen who were not particularly well educated. The new popular piety, the new intensity of religious feeling, were first expressed in Latin writings which have remained a model for devotional works down to the present day. No one has ever expressed the ideal of Christian love or the obligations of Christian morality better than did St. Bernard; his work has influenced even the most radical Protestant sects. Just as important are the Latin hymns of the twelfth century. Not only are they still sung in our churches (for example, *Jerusalem the Golden*) but they also mark an important technical shift in the art of poetry. They are the first great examples of the rhymed, rhythmic verse which was gradually replacing the quantitative metres of classical literature.

Another group of Latin writers lies at the opposite extreme from the religious leaders, and reminds us once more how many-sided the twelfth century was. These are the Goliardic poets, who had little respect for the conventions of their own age, but who could make Latin sing in a way that few men have equaled. Most of them were wandering students, more interested in this world than in studying about the next one, more anxious to demonstrate their cleverness than their scholarship. They wrote good-humored begging songs, bitter satires against the luxury of worldly prelates, hilarious rhymes for drinking-bouts, perfect little poems on the coming of spring, and love-songs which are sometimes tender and sometimes lustful. Some of their most characteristic work was translated by Symonds in *Wine, Women, and Song,* and the success of his translation shows how much closer they were to modern forms of expression than to the classical spirit.

Even more widely known in the twelfth century were the works of the vernacular poets. Here French writers took the lead, although they were soon followed by Germans and by Italians. First came the *chansons de geste,* brief epics of feudal warfare. They praise the feudal virtues—generosity, loyalty to one's lord, bravery, unceasing combat against the infidel. They have little to say about women or romantic love, but they portray the emotions and thoughts of the military class with surprising skill. When does bravery turn into foolhardiness? when does mistreatment by a lord justify rebellion by a vassal?—such are the problems which they raise. The greatest of the *chansons*—the *Song of Roland*—added a new gallery of heroes to European literature. Roland, Oliver, and their peers are at least as well known as Ulysses and Aeneas.

Soon after the *chansons de geste,* French writers began to revive the old Celtic legends, the stories of King Arthur and his knights, of Perceval and the Grail, of Tristan and Isolde. Pure adventure, magic and enchantment, and, above all, the overwhelming and tragic power of love were the chief themes of the Celtic stories. Some of this material, such as the tale of Tristan and Isolde, could not easily be reconciled with Christian morality, but, Christian or not, it tremendously stimulated the European imagination and has fascinated poets ever since. Writers in every country seized upon it and elaborated it, sometimes merely an escape literature, sometimes as the source for great poems. Curiously enough the Germans, with little Celtic background, did as well with these stories as the French; one of the finest versions of the Perceval legend is by the German, Wolfram von Eschenbach.

Chansons de geste and Celtic legend were products of northern France, at least in their first forms. The South did little with this material; it concentrated on lyric poetry. This was the great century of Provençal civilization—an age of flourishing towns, wealthy nobles, and a refined, almost artificial, social life. The troubadours wrote for this gay and sophisticated society; they expressed its hopes and fears in intensely personal form. They celebrated the joys of battle, they criticized or praised famous men, but their most typical and influential work was the love lyric. Often they were merely ingenious, over-proud of intricate rhyme-schemes or elaborate similes, but at their best they expressed real emotion in perfect form. They were soon imitated by poets of other countries; most medieval lyrics can be traced back, more or less directly, to Provençal forms.

The writers of the twelfth century created a new tradition in European literature, a tradition which was to compete with that of the classical period for centuries. New subject matter, new themes and new techniques had been introduced, never to be forgotten. For all their classical training, Renaissance writers re-told the stories of Arthur and Roland in the rhymed verse of the Middle Ages. The romantic movement of the early nineteenth century was accompanied by revived interest in medieval litera-ture. The imagination of European peoples has been repeatedly stimulated by the marvelous stories which were first written down in the twelfth century.

Among the new themes of twelfth-century writers were those of courtesy and romantic love. No one can argue that love, or even courtesy, were invented in the twelfth century, but it might be claimed that men of the twelfth century were somewhat prouder of their courtesy and much more interested in their love-affairs than their immediate ancestors. It is easy to understand why they took courtesy so seriously. Just emerging from an age of

violence and easy warfare, the only alternative to good manners
was a battle. It is not quite so easy to understand the great importance which romantic love rather suddenly acquired. Among
the upper classes, marriage was a business transaction, the one
business transaction which even the most impractical nobleman
understood. The best wife was the one who had the biggest
dowry—age, beauty, and character were unimportant if the
woman had extensive lands. Once married, a good wife produced
male heirs, ran the household economically, and never contradicted
her husband. Men who were not satisfied with these businesslike
arrangements might have affairs with other women, but they were
seldom serious or long-lasting. There was nothing very romantic
about relations between men and women in the early Middle Ages.

The problem, then, is whether the emphasis on romantic love
in twelfth-century literature reflects a change in social behavior.
To some extent it does, but the amount of change can easily be
exaggerated. As we have seen, feudal warfare was being discouraged and the land-holding class was acquiring a little more
ready cash. With leisure and money, the upper classes sought new
amusements, or tried to get more pleasure out of old occupations.
Thus hunting became a sport instead of a necessity, and developed
elaborate rules and nomenclature. In the same way, fighting,
feasting, and love-making were formalized, and the physical acts
were surrounded by elaborate ceremonies.

This new ceremonious behavior—chivalry, courtliness, courtly
love—first appeared in southwestern France, in the duchy of
Aquitaine. Some scholars think that it was a result of Moorish
influence, and it is true that among the Moslems of Spain we find
lyrics not unlike those of the troubadours, some emphasis on
courtly love, and some examples of chivalric behavior among the
military class. It is also true that the nobility of southern France
was more interested in pleasure and less concerned with affairs of
government than that of the northern provinces. Aquitaine was
less well organized, much more loosely administered than Nor-

mandy or Flanders, and the nobles of the region had more time for their amusements. In any case, the new type of upper-class social behavior originated there, and spread slowly throughout the rest of Western Europe. Northern France was not affected until the end of the twelfth century, England and Germany not until well into the thirteenth century.

The new code was incomplete and artificial, but it slowly wrought important changes in European society. It did impose some restraints on a class with great power; it did insist on formalities which blunted bad temper and passion. Although the chivalric ideals of loyalty, honor, respect for a worthy opponent, and protection of the weak were not always observed, especially in dealing with inferiors, they were a sufficient improvement on earlier practices to gain the support of the Church. They led, very gradually, to some mitigation of the horrors of warfare. Even more important, the modern idea of the gentleman grew directly out of the medieval ideas of chivalry and courtesy. When the military class ceased to be merely a bodyguard of tough warriors, when it began to take an interest in social accomplishments, an important transformation had taken place. It is true that these social accomplishments did not yet demand a high degree of education—that was to come with the Renaissance—but they did include some knowledge of music, vernacular poetry, history, and local law. The ruling class was becoming civilized, and while it acquired new vices with its new virtues, it was at least outgrowing the ignorant brutality of earlier times.

The effect of these new ideas on the position of women demands special consideration. Marriage remained a business affair, completely outside the scope of courtly love. The new concept of romantic love, expressed in the lyrics of the troubadours and the acts of chivalrous knights, applied almost entirely to extra-marital relations. It was doubtless an improvement when knights courted their mistresses instead of violating their servant-girls, but this was scarcely a complete answer to the old problem of the relative status of the two sexes. And yet, while the idea of romantic love came in, so to speak, at the back door, it did spread gradually beyond its early limits. If some women were to be worshipped as almost divine and served faithfully for years, why not all? If love determined the choice of a mistress, why not that of a wife? The growth of these ideas can be easily traced in European literature, as it develops the theme of the eternal opposition between the young who want to marry for love, and the old who put first family, status, and wealth.

It is also true that chivalry, at its best, demanded special consideration for the weak (and therefore, for women) and that the cult of the Virgin reflected some respect on the female sex as a whole. The two forces worked together; St. Francis was not the only religious figure who used the language of chivalry to express his devotion to Our Lady. Yet these factors affected only women of the upper classes, and even this privileged group was far from being emancipated in the twelfth, or even in the thirteenth century. They had a wider and more amusing social life, but legally and practically they were still subordinated to their husbands and fathers.

The work of the twelfth century which is best known today is probably its art. The new Gothic style, which has influenced so many churches and college buildings of our own time, was developed in the middle years of the century, and with the new style in architecture came equally important innovations in the other arts. Nowhere else are the basic characteristics of the twelfth century more apparent—its energy and originality, its desire for richer expression of its ideas, and its deep religious feeling. At the beginning of the century Romanesque architecture was reaching its climax. Derived, at long remove, from Roman forms, it was a sober, restrained, and practical style. Its model had been the basilica, or Roman law-court, a long room, divided into three aisles by pillars which held up the roof. Something had been done to modify the severity of the design by adding a circular

apse, or a round of chapels, back of the altar, and by introducing
transepts in front of the altar, thus giving the whole building the
shape of a cross. Yet while the best Romanesque churches were
very beautiful, they did not satisfy the men of the twelfth century.
With their heavy rounded arches and predominantly horizontal
lines they seemed too earthbound, too finite. They did not express
the new piety which soared toward heaven, which veiled everything in tender mysticism, which thought in terms of the infinite.
Just as men turned from classical models in literature to seek new
forms, so did they turn from the classical style and its derivatives
in architecture.

The first experiments in the new style took place in north
France, especially in the region around Paris. One of the earliest
examples was the monastery church of St. Denis, built by the
great abbot Suger in the first half of the century. We are fortunate
in having Suger's own description of the work; it is evident that
what he sought above everything else was light and color. These
qualities, to Suger, had mystical significance; they were the direct
reflection of the divine spirit. In seeking more light, the roof was
raised, the windows were enlarged and the walls were reduced to
a bare minimum. The weight of the roof was concentrated on a
few points in the upper walls by rib-vaulting, and these points
were reinforced by external buttresses. The main lines of the
building became vertical instead of horizontal and the clear-cut
outlines of the Romanesque style were softened. A Romanesque
church was sharply separated from surrounding space; a Gothic
church merged with it. Both inside and out, the eye was carried
onward and upward until it sought the infinite.

These changes did not take place all at once; the first Gothic
architects were a little hesitant about pushing their new ideas to
the limit. And yet the new style developed with amazing rapidity,
unhampered by the conservatism which is supposed to be typical
of the Middle Ages. Romanesque style was obsolete in the Île de
France within a half-century of the first experiments. In the next

half-century some of the most perfect Gothic churches in existence—Chartres and Paris—had been built. We do not move much
more rapidly today; it took us just about the same length of time
to develop and perfect the architectural ideas made possible by
the invention of the building with a steel skeleton.

The other arts were also associated with religion and with the
building of churches. Color was desired as well as light, so the
windows were filled with stained glass. The cathedrals had to be
decorated, so the façades and porches were filled with sculptured
figures. But stained glass and sculpture had a double function—
instruction as well as ornamentation. The church building was the
Bible of the illiterate; windows and portals told the familiar stories
of Christ and the saints. This was not realistic art, though medieval
craftsmen could be realistic enough in minor details of flowers
and shrubbery. But in their major figures they were trying to tell
a story or convey an idea. Figures became symbols; there was no
attempt to make them lifelike or to achieve the ideal beauty of
the Greeks. Yet, by concentrating on the idea or the emotion
which was to be portrayed, the artists attained a new type of
beauty. It is a beauty based on faith and knowledge; it can be appreciated only after study, but the study is well worth while.

4

The Medieval Summer

THE CATHEDRAL OF REIMS

1. THE TEMPER OF THE THIRTEENTH CENTURY

THE GREAT French historian, Marc Bloch, has reminded us that centuries are merely artificial measuring devices, created by the human mind for its own convenience, and that there is no reason why we should expect a measuring-rod to have a life and character of its own. He is right, in general, and yet there are centuries which seem to correspond, roughly, to clearly marked stages of historical development. Such a century was the twelfth, the springtime of medieval civilization. The seed had been sown earlier, but good seed had been wasted before, and no one in the last half of the eleventh century could have predicted the amazing growth which came after 1100, a flowering of civilization after a long winter of violence and frustration. The thirteenth century has a less distinct character. Just as the transition from spring to summer is more gradual and less perceptible than that from winter to spring, so the civilization of the thirteenth century grew naturally and easily out of that of the twelfth, without striking changes in aims or methods. No one, looking at a Romanesque church of 1000, could have foreseen Suger's church of St. Denis, but anyone looking at St. Denis could have made a fairly good guess about the course of ecclesiastical architecture for the next century. The same situation prevailed in other types of human activity; the basic patterns were devised in the twelfth century, while the thirteenth century merely filled in details.

And yet this very lack of originality and love of detail helps to distinguish the work of the thirteenth century from that of its predecessor. If there were fewer new ideas, there was more care in expressing the ideas which had already been acquired. Men of the thirteenth century were not satisfied with the rough approximations and bold outlines of the earlier period. They wanted everything to fall into a logical, well-organized, complete pattern, whether they were dealing with legal formulae, the articles of faith, or the structure of a church. They were troubled by discrepancies, contradictions, and omissions which men of the twelfth century had taken in their stride. As a result, some of the finest products of medieval civilization came from the thirteenth century. The ideas were still fresh, and yet men had had enough experience with them to smooth out the rough spots and perfect the details.

Reason, logic, law—these were key words of the thirteenth century. These qualities had been stressed in the educational revival of the twelfth century, and it was natural enough for them to become prominent in a society which was employing thousands of university graduates in key positions in Church and State. And yet rationalism and legalism were not confined to the educated class and were not due entirely to the rise of the universities. Many rulers, some nobles, and most of the business class shared these ideas. This was certainly due, in part, to the fact that the thirteenth century was a relatively peaceful period in Western Europe and that men who could not settle their disputes by fighting turned to the rational processes of the law as the best substitute. More important, the men of the thirteenth century were convinced that reason, logic, and law were inherent in the structure of the world, because they were derived directly from God. Everything would make sense, everything could be fitted into a pattern with a little more effort. Men of the thirteenth century believed, as strongly as those of the eighteenth century, that the effort should be made.

As has already been suggested, the thirteenth century was a relatively stable period. The prevailing rationalism and legalism were both a result and a cause of this stability. For example, it was easier to be precise about class distinctions because no new class erupted through the crust of society as the bourgeoisie had done in the twelfth century. On the other hand, precision and legal definition sharpened class distinctions and decreased social mobility. It was easier to tell who was noble and who was not in 1300 than in 1200; for that very reason, it became more difficult to move into the ruling class. In the same way, the long struggle of the bourgeoisie for recognition as a separate class was practically won by the middle of the century, and almost immediately the bourgeoisie began to close ranks and make it difficult for a peasant to secure full rights of citizenship in the towns. Just as there was social stability, so there was a large degree of economic stability. The great boom of the twelfth century gradually leveled off into a moderate but continuing prosperity. Western Europe certainly increased in wealth, productivity, and population, but there were no spectacular gains such as had marked the earlier period, and at the end of the century there were even signs of approaching economic stagnation. As a result, there was a growing tendency among all classes to avoid risks and to prize security, to seek a comfortable niche in the existing economic and social structure rather than to attempt to change the structure.

The slowing down of the rate of expansion, the gradual lessening of opportunity, the concentration on immediate advantages, slowly ate away the exuberant energy which had marked the twelfth century. Men were somewhat less willing to start new ventures or to embark on big projects. Whether it was the building of a new cathedral or the settlement of a new province, the investigation of a new branch of knowledge or the opening of a new trade-route, if the work were not well advanced before the middle of the century, the chances were that it would not be finished. Thus there developed an attitude of caution, even of worldly-wiseness, which is quite noticeable in the last years of the century. Cleverness became the chief virtue and stupidity the greatest sin. Full commitment to an ideal seemed a little naïve; the prudent man knew how to guard his own interests while obeying the letter of the law. The change is nicely illustrated in the career of the famous historian Joinville. The young

Joinville, in the 1240's, went on Crusade without question; the middle-aged Joinville, in the 1260's, thought it wiser to stay home to look after his property.

What of the Church in a century which became more rationalistic, more legalistic, more cautious and earthbound with every decade? Obviously the Christian ideals, which had played such an important rôle in the building of medieval civilization, were threatened. As we shall see, the Church struggled valiantly to maintain these ideals, but the Church itself was affected by the temper of the times. With administration in the hands of canon lawyers and doctrine in the hands of theologians trained in Aristotelian logic, there was a coldness in action and a dryness in thought which lessened the sympathy between the high officials of the Church and the people of Europe. St. Bernard had been able to combine the rôle of an ecclesiastical statesman with that of a leader of popular piety, but there was no St. Bernard in the thirteenth century. Instead there was a growing division between those who could run the complex machinery of the Church and those who could appeal to the emotions of the people.

And yet the difficulty was not entirely with the leadership of the Church. The people of Europe had enjoyed increasing prosperity for several generations; they had become more and more interested in the secular activities which seemed to assure that prosperity. They meant to remain good Christians; they repented in tears and in terror when popular preachers denounced their worldliness. But, for all their good intentions, they found it difficult to put religion ahead of their own interests, or to accept the leadership of the Church when secular leaders were urging other policies. The influence of the Church, still great when the century opened, had declined seriously before it ended. Not that the Church had lost all authority, but it was beginning to lose its position of unquestioned leadership, its ability to set the basic standards and goals of society. It was beginning to face formidable competition for men's loyalty from secular governments; it was beginning to suffer from the dry rot of formalism, indifference, and hypocrisy. This decline in religious influence was just commencing in the thirteenth century and the first evidences of an independent secular culture were appearing only sporadically. But even this stage of beginnings affected the temper of the thirteenth century and clearly distinguished it from that of the twelfth.

II. THE PAPAL MONARCHY—INNOCENT III

Innocent III (1198–1216) was one of the great medieval popes, perhaps the greatest. Under him the leadership of the Church reached its highest point; he was the arbiter of all disputes, the court of last resort in all controversies. Under him the administration of the Church was improved and the law of the Church was clarified. He suppressed a dangerous heresy in southern France; he started a new wave of popular piety by encouraging the founders of the Franciscan and Dominican orders. Yet his brilliant pontificate created new problems for the Church. The extension of papal leadership brought new responsibilities and new vulnerabilities. The means he used to increase the power and improve the administration of the Church in the long run injured its moral position and its prestige. The policies to which he committed the Church led to the humiliation of the papacy at the end of the century.

When Innocent became pope in 1198, his first concern was with the political situation in Italy and Germany. The emperor Henry VI, who had just died, had put the papacy in a difficult position. Henry was well obeyed in Germany, ruled Tuscany and central Italy through his German army commanders, and held Sicily and Naples through his marriage to Constance, heiress of the Norman kings. The pope in Rome was completely surrounded by imperial territory; most of the Italian lands claimed by the pope were occupied by imperial troops. Innocent felt insecure; he wanted to acquire a solid block of territory in central Italy and to separate the kingdom of Sicily from the Empire. He was successful in both policies. Taking advantage of the confusion which followed the emperor's death, he drove out the German administrators and established his own authority in central Italy. He was the real creator of the Papal States, that wavering band of territory which separated north and south Italy for centuries. At the same time, he supported the claims of the infant Frederick II (son of Henry VI) to Sicily, while encouraging the German princes to choose someone else as emperor. To make sure that Rome and the area around Rome would not again be caught in a pincers, he demanded that each candidate for the Empire renounce all his claims to central and southern Italy. This requirement encouraged a civil war in Germany, and when the pro-papal candidate finally won he promptly violated his pledge by claiming part of the Papal States. Innocent replied by sending Frederick II to conquer Germany. The strategy, for the moment, was completely successful. Frederick, as heir of the great Hohenstaufen line, was popular in Germany and secured the crown with little difficulty. In return for Innocent's support, he promised to give Sicily to his son, to renounce his claims to lands in central Italy, and to aid papal policy by going on a Crusade. Thus Innocent had freed Rome from encirclement, and had apparently changed the Empire from an enemy to an ally.

Yet his success was not without its dangers. Innocent cannot be blamed for failing to foresee that Frederick would not keep his word; no one could yet tell how the young king's character would develop. But Innocent had committed the Church to the dangerous proposition that its safety depended on certain political arrangements—on a weak and subservient Empire, a disunited Italy, and a relatively large and independent Papal State. Innocent had good reason to think that this situation was advantageous to the Church, and yet it was a grave mistake to tie a religious organization, the guardian of eternal truth, to a temporary political settlement. Because Innocent had established the policy, succeeding popes fought desperately and unscrupulously to preserve the Papal States and to prevent the rise of a strong power in Italy. Their concentration on this political problem and their use of spiritual authority to preserve political advantages weakened the prestige of the Church and gave its enemies material for damaging attacks.

Innocent, like all great administrators, had the ability to work on many problems simultaneously. He did not allow himself to be absorbed by difficulties in Germany and Italy; he wanted to protect the interests of the Church wherever they were threatened. But in these other areas he showed the same tendency to rely on military and political combinations. For example, when King John of England refused to accept a papal nominee as archbishop of Canterbury, Innocent was too impatient to rely entirely on the slow process of stirring up public opinion through spiritual penalties against the disobedient ruler. He tried excommunication and interdict, but when they failed to produce quick results he encouraged the king of France to plan an invasion of England. This threat produced quick results; John not only accepted the pope's candidate as archbishop, but even surrendered his kingdom to Innocent and received it back as a fief of the Church.

Innocent reacted in the same way to the danger caused by the rapid growth of heresy in south France. The clergy of this region had lost control of their flocks, partly through their own faults, partly through the influence of able and persuasive heretical leaders. The Waldensian heresy, founded by a pious layman of Lyons who was annoyed by the ignorance and incompetence of the clergy, developed a creed which retained Christian doctrine but rejected the sacraments and the organization of the Church. The much more dangerous Albigensian heresy was not even Christian in doctrine. The Albigensians had accepted a curious dualistic religion, probably imported from the East, which was based on the old idea of a perpetual conflict between the gods of good and evil. Jehovah was really Satan, the god of evil; he was responsible for the death of Jesus, who had been sent to save men by the god of good. Everything material had been created by the god of evil; therefore, the leaders of the heresy rejected all worldly ties and lived lives of extreme asceticism. Their intense faith and rigid standards of morality impressed the rather worldly people of the western Mediterranean basin. Their doctrine appealed to people who had long been taught that the world was evil and who wondered how a benevolent and omnipotent god could have created such an unhappy place. The heretics called themselves the "Cathari" (the "purified"); others often referred to them as the "good men." They gained thousands of followers in north Italy and Spain, but were most numerous in south France, in the region around Toulouse, Carcassonne, and Albi (whence the name, Albigensian). There they had organized a rival church, with their own clergy and ritual; there they had the support, or at least the neutrality, of many feudal lords.

The Church had been worried about the Albigensians for at least half a century; earlier popes had tried to convert the heretics by sending famous preachers among them, and had negotiated with local lords to make them withdraw their support. Innocent continued and intensified these activities without marked success. He was already growing impatient, when the murder of a papal legate by heretics gave him an excuse for abandoning methods of peaceful persuasion. In effect, he declared war on the heretics and their supporters, and summoned the army of the Church—the Crusade—to suppress them. The kings and princes of Europe were not entirely sure that Innocent's policy was wise, but the sincerely pious—and poor—nobles of north France saw an opportunity to gain salvation and wealth at the same time. Under the leadership of Simon de Montfort they invaded the south, and defeated the Albigensians and their allies in a long, bloody, and difficult war. The heresy was not wiped out, but it was driven underground. The boldest heretics had been killed, and lords who had been sympathetic to the heretics were replaced by orthodox barons of the north. There could be no more open resistance, and the Church was soon to organize its special tribunal of the Inquisition to root out the concealed heretics.

The Albigensian Crusade accomplished its purpose, but even in Innocent's eyes it was not an unqualified success. Many sincere Catholics of the south were angered by the invasion of the north French barons; some of them were so angered that they died fighting on the side of the heretics. The most conspicuous victim was the entirely orthodox king of Aragon, who had distinguished himself in a great victory over the Moors of Spain only a year before he was killed by the army of Simon de Montfort. For the king of Aragon, the Albigensian Crusade was merely an unjust war of conquest, and there were thousands of other Catholics who shared his views. The Church was permanently weakened in south France; it is no accident that Protestants were especially numerous in that region three centuries later.

In addition, Innocent had unwittingly weakened the unity of the Christian Commonwealth. The people of Western Europe had been bound together by a common foreign policy directed against a common enemy, the Moslems. Now the chief implement of that foreign policy, the Crusade, had been directed against one part of Western Europe for the benefit of another part. It was becoming a divisive instead of a unifying force. It might be argued that heretics had put themselves outside the European Commonwealth, but Innocent used the Crusade at least once, possibly twice, against men who were certainly orthodox, even if disobedient to the pope. He proclaimed a Crusade against a faction in Sicily which was opposing his policy there; he probably promised Crusade privileges to the king of France when he used the threat of a French invasion to bring John of England to terms. It was a dangerous precedent to combine the Crusade with political maneuvers within Europe; unfortunately it was a precedent followed by later popes.

While Innocent could use the Crusade for his policy in Europe, he lost control of the one overseas Crusade which took place during his pontificate. A group of French and Italian barons planned to sail from Venice in 1202 to regain Jerusalem, which had been in Saracen hands since 1187. They overestimated their numbers and resources, as medieval barons usually did, and arrived in Venice without enough men to fill or pay for the ships which they had hired. The Venetians showed no desire to sacrifice their profits to their ideals; instead they suggested that the Crusaders work off their debt by capturing Zara, a Christian city on the Adriatic which was a trade rival of Venice. In spite of Innocent's protests Zara was taken, and worse was to follow. Instead of proceeding directly to the Holy Land, the Venetians produced a claimant to the throne of the Byzantine Empire and argued most of the Crusaders into attacking Constantinople. They urged, with some logic, that a friendly emperor in Constantinople could give great assistance to an army in Palestine; they said nothing about the trade advantages which Venice could expect from such a change. Constantinople should have been impregnable, but the government had been weakened by a series of palace revolutions, and the Crusaders took the city in 1204 without much trouble. Then, as might have been expected, they quarreled with their protégé, the new emperor, drove him from his throne, and established a Latin Empire of the East which lasted until 1261.

Innocent had officially opposed these developments, but he was faced with an accomplished fact, and had to make the best of it. After all, the Greek Church was schismatic, though not heretical —that is, while its doctrine was sound it rejected papal supremacy. Here was a chance to reunite the Churches and to bring all Eastern Christians under papal control. This was a great gain, far outweighing the postponement of an expedition against Jerusalem. The Crusaders were forgiven, and a Latin hierarchy was appointed to guide the Greeks and Slavs into the papal fold.

Had the Latin Empire been strong, this would have been sound politics, if not good morality. But the Latin Empire was never a success. Outlying provinces rebelled and became independent under Byzantine princes. The Bulgarians held most of the Balkans and threatened Constantinople. The Crusading leaders each sought to establish an autonomous principality and seldom combined against their common enemies. The real result of the establishment of the Latin Empire was a fatal weakening of the defenses of Europe in the East. Though the Byzantine Empire was restored in 1261, it never regained all its old territory or strength. In its weakened state, it could do no more than conduct a long rear-guard action against the Turks, who began their attack on South-eastern Europe in the fourteenth century. Ifs are always dangerous in history, but one cannot help wondering what would have happened if the Fourth Crusade had captured a Moslem instead of a Christian capital.

Innocent had studied canon law at Bologna, the great school for judges and administrators. He seems to have enjoyed this side of his work, and anyone who reads the registers of his pontificate is amazed by the amount of business done at the papal court. Innocent was a first-rate administrator; he knew how to delegate authority while keeping control over all major policy decisions. By seizing every opportunity to intervene in local disputes, he greatly increased papal control over the Church. For example, all disputed elections of bishops were referred to his court; Innocent often quashed the claims of both parties and then imposed his own candidate. Innocent set high standards for the clergy and was reasonably successful in enforcing them, thanks to his administrative ability and his clarification of canon law. He completed this part of his work in a great Church Council, which met in the Lateran in 1215 to sum up and codify the reforms which he had made. But the more the pope did, the more complex and expensive the administration of the Church became. Appeals to the pope multiplied and orders to investigate the reasons for appeal rained down on local prelates. No one could become a bishop without justifying his election to the pope; no one could remain a bishop without defending his policies at the papal court. As a result, every church official had to increase his staff of administrative and legal experts. This in turn forced the higher clergy to insist on the rigorous collection of every penny which they felt was due them, and so the old complaints about the avarice of the clergy became more frequent and more bitter.

Innocent solved his own financial problems chiefly through efficient collection of well-established revenues, but he set a dangerous precedent by imposing an income tax on the clergy in 1199. It is true that the tax was only 2½ per cent and that it was for a laudable purpose, the relief of the Holy Land. But, once the example had been set, later popes could raise the rate (sometimes to 20 per cent) and change the purpose. Even worse, lay rulers began to feel that it was as legitimate for them to tax the clergy to support their policies, as for the pope to tax them to support his. So heavier and heavier burdens were imposed on the clergy, and their natural reaction was to become even more concerned about careful administration of their properties and revenues. It was a good system for producing lawyers and men of business; it was not so well adapted to producing spiritual leaders.

The clergy, however, were far from being entirely to blame for the declining idealism of the thirteenth century. As we have seen, there was even greater concern with material prosperity among the laity; witness the ingenuity with which the Venetians had increased their trade through a Crusade. The mendicant orders of friars were founded under Innocent III to combat the growing worldliness of both clergy and laity, and it says much for the pope's breadth of vision that he was willing to sanction a reform movement which criticized, if only by example, his own preoccupation with politics and administration. It is also significant that the founders of both orders—St. Francis and St. Dominic—found in the end that their most necessary function was preaching to common laymen, though each had begun his work with other purposes in mind. The clergy were too busy, and the best of them too remote from ordinary life, to give laymen the guidance which they craved. The laity knew that they were drifting into patterns of living which were not fully in harmony with Christian ideals, and yet they found it hard to change these patterns. They could not ease their consciences with mere formal observance after the great awakening of popular piety in the preceding century. They were eager for religious teaching which would deal with individual problems and demand individual participation; if they could not satisfy these desires in the Catholic Church they were apt to turn to heretics for help. The mendicant orders, in their best days, answered all these needs; their rapid growth shows how serious the problem was.

St. Dominic was a Spaniard, an educated clergyman, who was shocked by the prevalence of heresy in south France. His first idea was to establish a monastery in the heart of heretical territory, but he soon saw that more active measures were needed. He gradually developed an order of preaching friars—men who were bound by the usual monastic vows, but who traveled constantly through the countryside, combatting false doctrine and preaching the true faith. The Dominicans were, at first, a more scholarly order than the Franciscans; they soon acquired a strong position in the universities and had excellent schools of their own. They appealed more to the intellect than to the emotions; they explained how the new activities of the thirteenth century could be made to conform to the old faith. Yet the ordinary Dominican was not so intellectual that he could not appeal to the common man, and the Dominicans played an important rôle in the religious revivals which swept through Europe in the thirteenth century.

St. Francis was an Italian, an almost uneducated layman, whose father was a wealthy merchant. He found his vocation, not through observing the heresies of others, but through disgust with his own behavior. Rich, worldly, and gay, he had dreamed of becoming a knight, but a serious illness destroyed his hopes. He then began to examine his ambitions, and found that he could not reconcile them with his faith. He wanted to follow the Gospel precepts literally, to live in absolute poverty as the servant of all. Other men with similar convictions gathered around him, and he found that he had founded a religious order almost without planning it. He longed to retire from the world, but his fame spread through Italy and town after town begged for his presence. Here was a man who lived religion instead of talking about it, whose personal influence was so great that the boldest sinners yielded to his commands. Like St. Dominic he soon found that his real mission was to preach to laymen, especially to the troubled laymen of the Italian towns who, like himself, found it hard to reconcile their religious ideals with their desires for worldly success. His order grew rapidly and had spread throughout Western Europe by his death in 1226.

If the Dominicans appealed to the intellect, the Franciscans appealed to the emotions. This is, of course, an oversimplification; some Franciscans were great theologians, just as some Dominicans were great revivalists. Yet it is true that the Franciscans, as a group, cared little about schools and nice points of doctrine, and tried to convince their hearers by giving them a sense of sin rather than by intellectual arguments. They stimulated and revived popular piety; they damped down the immoderate desires for wealth and power which were so strong among laymen of the thirteenth century. The fact that the Church preserved its position of leadership until the last quarter of the century, in spite of growing competition with secular interests, is due in great part to the work of the Franciscans.

Thanks to the Dominicans and Franciscans, heresy was weakened, worldliness and indifference were checked, and the intellectual and emotional appeal of the faith was strengthened. But the achievements of the friars were an indictment of other members of the clergy. The monks were supposed to set examples of holy living; the prelates were supposed to instruct and inspire the faithful and to combat heresy; the faculties of the universities were to teach theology and Christian philosophy. There was, quite naturally, jealousy of the friars among all these groups, and it took repeated orders from the popes to establish the right of the friars to preach and teach everywhere. Such professional quarrels did not help the prestige of the Church, and the mendicant orders were not unmarked by the conflict. The successors of St. Dominic and St. Francis showed a tendency to make their orders conform to old monastic standards in order to avoid criticism; they discouraged the old wandering, begging life and built convents in which the friars were expected to spend most of their time. This irritated the more zealous friars, who wanted to imitate the founding saints in every detail, and so new quarrels broke out within the orders. At the same time, the original enthusiasm aroused by the friars among laymen was declining. Any generation has only so much emotional capital, and when it is spent a period of indifference is apt to follow. The friars had used up a great deal of this capital in repeated bursts of revivalism, and the second or third generation to whom they preached was less influenced by them than the first. They remained useful members of the Church, but they could not play a decisive rôle in the new crises which developed as the century drew near its end.

III. THE PAPAL MONARCHY—THE POPES AND THE HOHENSTAUFEN

When Innocent III died, he had a right to feel that he had at least freed the papacy from the threat of domination by a secular ruler. Rome was protected by the broad belt of Papal States; Germany was ruled by Frederick II, a papal protégé; Sicily was to be handed over to Frederick's infant son, who would presumably be in papal wardship. The only flaw in these arrangements was that Innocent had completely misunderstood the character of Frederick II. He must have known that Frederick was a youth of unusual ability—intelligent, well-educated, energetic, bold, with a real talent for politics and administration. He had every reason to hope that Frederick would be grateful to the Church which had first preserved his Sicilian heritage and then set him on the throne of the Empire. But what he failed to see was that Frederick was overwhelmingly ambitious, determined to be a real Roman Emperor, that he incarnated all those desires for worldly wealth and power which were so prevalent in the thirteenth century, that he could not be bound by benefits or restrained by religious scruples. Frederick was no heretic—that would have required more faith than he possessed—he was simply a politician. The Church, to him, was a political force, to be treated in exactly the same way as other political forces. He would negotiate with it, as an equal, as long as he could, and when it became necessary he would fight it in order to get a satisfactory settlement. If the welfare of the Church depended on the preservation of Innocent's political settlement and if that settlement, in turn, depended on the good-will of Frederick II, then the future was dark.

It took some time for the popes to realize that Frederick was dangerous. The emperor could be plausible and ingratiating when he wished, and Innocent's immediate successor was not very energetic. He scolded Frederick for neither giving up Sicily nor going on a Crusade, as he had promised, but took no decisive action. The next pope, Gregory IX (1227-1241), was less complacent. He ordered Frederick to start a Crusade, and excommunicated him when he failed to set out on time. Then Frederick completely confused public opinion by going to Palestine and regaining Jerusalem through a treaty with the Sultan of Egypt, who was quite ready to surrender a distant outpost in return for peace with the Christians. Frederick's behavior was shrewd rather than heroic and his hold on Jerusalem was precarious (the city was lost again in 1244). Nevertheless, he had succeeded where the greatest kings of the West had failed, and the pope's attack on him was made to seem rather silly. A peace was patched up, and pope and emperor remained on fairly good terms for the next few years.

The struggle broke out again over the question of the cities of north Italy. Frederick wanted to control these towns, both because of their wealth and because they could block the roads to Germany, from which he drew his best troops. The pope opposed this policy for obvious reasons; it renewed the old threat of encirclement and was directed against municipalities which had been faithful allies of the papacy. The situation was made worse by the fact that almost every town was split by political feuds, so that if one faction looked to the emperor for assistance the other was sure to turn to the pope. Thus even a small success in north Italy was apt to stir up a large amount of trouble, and Frederick won a great success. In 1237 he completely defeated the army of a league of north Italian cities at Cortenuova, and for a few weeks the whole region was at his mercy.

The fears of Gregory IX and his allies were not allayed by Frederick's actions after his victory. He refused to grant his opponents reasonable terms of peace; he announced his victory to the people of Rome in terms which suggested that he, and not the pope, was the ruler of the city. Perhaps he thought he could terrify his adversaries; instead he drove them to desperate resistance. Gregory formed an alliance with the emperor's enemies in north Italy, and soon gave the war against Frederick the name and character of a Crusade. When war proved indecisive, Gregory called a Council at Rome to take action against the emperor. Frederick, in one of the most audacious actions of his life, sent a fleet to attack the ships bearing members of the Council to Rome. The operation was entirely successful—too successful for Frederick's own good. He drowned or captured so many prelates that the Council could not take place, but he did this at the price of perpetual war with the Church. Up to this time there had been many churchmen who felt that Gregory's intransigence was as much to blame as Frederick's ambition, and who were working for another compromise peace. Now Frederick had transformed a private war with a particular pope into an attack on the Church Universal, and compromise was no longer possible. One side or the other had to win a complete victory.

Frederick had a brief breathing spell when Gregory died in

1241, for the cardinals found it hard to agree, and a new pope, Innocent IV, was not elected until 1243. Innocent was just as determined to check Frederick as Gregory had been, and he was more skillful as a politician. He established himself at Lyons, on the border of France, where neither the army nor the navy of Frederick could reach him. Then he called a General Council in 1245 which deposed Frederick from all his thrones—Germany, Sicily, and Jerusalem. Parchment depositions meant little, but Innocent used every means to stir up public opinion against the emperor and proclaimed Crusades against him in both Germany and Italy. Frederick was on the defensive for the last five years of his life, but he was never decisively defeated. He was still battling valiantly in Italy when he died in 1250.

The war against Frederick had been unedifying; it involved the pope in the scabrous details of Italian politics and still further cheapened the idea of the Crusade. Most European rulers showed no great enthusiasm for either side; Innocent IV received help only from those who saw a chance to profit from the confusion in Germany and Italy. But if the war was unedifying it was necessary—at least, if one accepts the papal argument that a united Italy under a strong ruler threatened the independence of the Church. The continuation of the war against Frederick's heirs is harder to justify. It is true that, given the strong medieval belief in rights of inheritance, any one of Frederick's descendants might have revived all his claims to power. It is true that the heads of the Church had been badly frightened, and that they felt that there was no safety as long as a Hohenstaufen ruled anywhere. But the bitter attacks on the "viper brood" and the continuation of the feud to the third and fourth generations did the Church infinite harm. The popes became even more involved in power politics, and their efforts to secure financial and military aid from lay rulers compromised the independence of the Church almost as badly as a Hohenstaufen victory would have done.

Innocent IV continued the Crusade against Frederick's son,

Conrad IV in both Germany and Italy. It was not difficult to keep Germany in turmoil, for Frederick had surrendered almost all his power in that country to the princes in order to have a free hand for the struggle in Italy. The Crusade against Conrad completed the destruction of imperial authority; Germany had no central government which amounted to anything from 1250 until the nineteenth century. Italy was a harder problem for the pope. Conrad held the kingdom of Sicily without much difficulty, and at his death in 1254 it passed to his illegitimate half-brother Manfred in spite of bitter papal opposition. Manfred could not be dislodged by threats or negotiations; finally the pope had to offer the kingdom to a French prince, Charles of Anjou. Charles demanded full Crusade benefits (forgiveness of sins and papal protection) and large sums of money from the Church before he would undertake the task. With this support he succeeded in defeating and killing Manfred in 1266, but Charles was barely established as king of Sicily when a new Hohenstaufen claimant appeared. This was Conradin, the young son of Conrad IV, who almost upset all papal plans for Italy before he was defeated in 1268. He had frightened both pope and king—how seriously is shown by the fact that he was executed in cold blood after he was captured. His death did not end the feud; in 1282 the people of the island of Sicily revolted against their French king and called in the ruler of Aragon, who had married a granddaughter of Frederick II. A new Crusade was proclaimed, this time against Aragon, but it was not successful. The Aragonese held the island of Sicily; the French dynasty retained Naples and the mainland; and the two families kept up an intermittent war until well into the fourteenth century.

The long struggle with Frederick II and his descendants forced the popes to behave more and more like secular monarchs. They had to raise armies, make alliances, and negotiate territorial agreements. They had to conduct propaganda campaigns against their enemies and justify their policies to their friends. Worst of all, they had to raise money. The income tax on the clergy, initiated by Innocent III, became almost an annual levy during the second half of the century at rates of from 10 to 20 per cent. Some of this money was used to support overseas Crusades, but by far the larger part of it was spent for the war against the Hohenstaufen. Often the tax was simply handed over to secular princes, who promised to fight for the papacy. The line between a tax given a king to pay for a political Crusade and a tax levied on the clergy by the same king for his own purposes was easy to cross, and by the end of the century the kings of France and England were imposing taxes on their clergy about two years out of three. The popes protested, but not too vigorously, because they felt that they might need the political support of these kings in the future. In short, through playing politics the popes had become politicians. They were no longer arbiters of the quarrels of European princes, for they had become involved in the quarrels themselves. As politicians they were influential and important, but they could be opposed and sometimes defeated by purely political weapons. Their prestige was lessened, their position of leadership was shaken, and the unity of the Commonwealth of Christendom was endangered by the weakness of its head.

During this period of war with the Hohenstaufen the popes completed their victory over their other great enemy, the Albigensian heretics. Simon de Montfort, who had led the first Crusade against the Albigensians, died soon after his victory, and his son was unable to hold the heretics in check. Louis VIII of France led a new Crusade against the Albigensians in 1225–26, and ended the threat of their military revival by placing the whole region under royal control. The heretics gave up their hopes of independent political existence, but they tried to preserve their faith through outward conformity and secret meetings. Crusades were useless in this new situation; some other means had to be devised to smoke out the hidden unbelievers. After a little experimentation, Gregory IX found the solution to the problem; he created the court of the Inquisition, and staffed it with learned and zealous Dominican friars.

The Inquisition had a difficult task; it had to discover the secret thoughts of men who were doing their best to conceal their beliefs. It had to use methods which we would condemn; it accepted hearsay evidence and believed that mere suspicion indicated some degree of guilt. In order to obtain convincing evidence it tried to force the accused to incriminate himself through tricky questioning, with torture as a last resort. It condemned many men to lifelong imprisonment for minor deviations from orthodoxy; it ordered secular rulers to burn stubborn heretics at the stake. But given the premises which most thirteenth-century men accepted, it was not completely unfair. If the soul is more important than the body, and if heresy kills the soul, then almost any action taken against heresy can be justified. In spite of the prejudice against heretics and the weighting of the procedure against the accused, the Inquisition honestly sought the truth as it saw the truth. Only a minority of its cases ended with a sentence of death; there were some acquittals and many moderate penalties. The worst period of the Inquisition came after heresy had been practically extirpated. Then spiteful neighbors avenged petty quarrels by denouncing their enemies as heretics; then fanatical Inquisitors, unable to find real enemies of the faith, invented charges of heresy to prove their zeal. The Inquisition also had a bad influence on the secular courts of the countries where it was established. Its procedure was so efficacious in producing convictions that it was imitated by secular judges. Continental courts relied heavily on self-incrimination and torture for centuries; England escaped this influence only because it was so orthodox that it never had an Inquisition.

IV. THE RISE OF THE SECULAR STATE

While the Church was destroying the Hohenstaufen monarchy, and weakening itself in the process, the kingdoms of the West were gaining strength and securing the loyalty of their subjects.

This was especially true of England and France, which had made great progress in the twelfth century, and which continued to lead all other European states in the thirteenth. A study of these two monarchies will illustrate most of the developments which took place in the whole group of Western kingdoms.

Philip Augustus, as we saw in the last chapter, had completely upset the balance of power that had long existed between the king of France and the great feudal lords. His conquests gave him far more territory than any vassal, and his new administrative system, based on *baillis* sent out from his court, gave him effective control of the men and resources of his newly acquired provinces. He had built a strong position and had made it secure. From his victory at Bouvines in 1214 to the end of the century no feudal rebellion had the slightest chance of success, and the great vassals learned that they must obey the king.

Philip Augustus had made the French monarchy strong, but he had not made it loved or respected. He had been unscrupulous himself—for example, in attacking the lands of Richard while the latter was crusading—and he had not punished unscrupulous agents. As long as his *baillis* kept their provinces under control Philip did not inquire too closely into their abuses of power. Philip had encouraged his officials to interfere with ecclesiastical courts, and his own reputation for piety was doubtful. He had been a lukewarm Crusader in Palestine and a neutral during the struggle against the Albigensian heretics. He had repudiated his lawful wife and contracted an illegal marriage; he had at times opposed the policies of Innocent III in England and in Germany. If the monarchy were to supplant the Church as the object of French loyalty, the kings would have to rival the clergy in moral character as well as in political power.

Philip's son and grandson added moral leadership to the physical predominance which their predecessor had attained. Louis VIII ruled only three years, 1223 to 1226, but he began the work of reforming the court and the administration. Even more important, he assumed leadership of the second phase of the Albigensian Crusade and thus strengthened the old alliance between the Church and the French monarchy. His territorial gains were equally important; he added most of the lands conquered from the heretics to the royal domain and prepared the way for the eventual annexation of all the south to the crown. Now the French king held a broad, central strip of land running from the Channel to the Mediterranean, and it became more difficult than ever before for rebellious vassals to combine against him.

Louis IX, the son of Louis VIII, was recognized as a saint by the Church shortly after his death. During his long reign (1226–1270) he gained a reputation for piety, honesty, and concern for the common welfare which surpassed that of most of the popes of his century. He inspired devotion to the French monarchy, devotion so strong that it survived all the disasters of the next century. For generations the "good times of St. Louis" were the standard by which all succeeding governments were measured.

He gained this reputation by his own personal uprightness and by his skill as an administrator. He set an example of piety and decency in his own life and he had a passion for justice which changed the whole tone of royal government. His *baillis* were far more honest than those of Philip Augustus, and he tried to prevent any backsliding by sending special investigating committees through the provinces to collect complaints against his officials. He heard many appeals for justice in person; when they became too numerous for him to deal with, he appointed some of his most trusted advisers to listen to any subject who came to ask help from his court. He could be fair to his enemies as well as to his friends. When he ended the long quarrel with England, which had begun when Philip seized John's lands, he made so many concessions that his councillors protested. By the middle of his reign he was the most respected king in Europe, and his attitude was often decisive in determining the policy of other rulers.

Besides all this, he was a Crusader, almost the only honest Crusader of his century. Everyone recognized that he was seeking only the recovery of the Holy Places, not his own profit. His first Crusade (1248–1254) was very nearly successful. He attacked Egypt in order to force the sultan to relinquish his outlying possession of Jerusalem, and was defeated only after he had captured an important Egyptian sea-port. Even this defeat did not discourage him; he spent the next three years strengthening the fortifications of the coastal towns which the Christians still held in Syria. His second Crusade (1270) was led astray by bad advice from King Charles of Sicily, and wasted its strength in an attack on Tunis. St. Louis died of fever on this expedition, a martyr to the faith in an age in which martyrdom was rare.

It is easy to see how this man raised the reputation of the French monarchy; it may be more difficult to understand how he made it strong. A pious ruler is not necessarily soft, and St. Louis wanted justice for himself as well as for his subjects. He would not take what was not his, but he would not surrender any of his rights, not even to the Church. And when it came to determining what were his rights, the final decision rested with royal courts or with the king himself. St. Louis was never deliberately unfair, and he tried to repress unfairness in his officials, but he did have a concept of kingship which forced him to expand his power. He believed that it was his duty to keep peace in his kingdom; he believed that his theoretical supremacy over all lesser lords should be an actual fact. To keep the peace he had to interfere with feudal autonomy; to make his theoretical overlordship real, he had to demand service and obedience from men who had never paid the slightest attention to the wishes of earlier kings. Prevailing political theory—even the theory of feudalism—supported him in these efforts, but there were many historical precedents against him. In the end he had his way because he had public opinion with him, because the extension of royal power meant an extension of peace and justice.

In increasing his power over the kingdom, St. Louis used legal procedures more than his father and grandfather had done. He did not have to conquer new territories; he could summon recalcitrant lords to Paris and make them accept the judgments of his court. With more business and more authority than it had had before, the court became better organized, more of a professional body. After 1250 it was known as the Parlement, and it was in the Parlement that cases involving royal rights were tried. Great barons still sat in the court, but the bulk of the work was done by men who had been trained in the royal administrative service. These men gradually worked out a jurisprudence favorable to the king; they insisted on his right to hear appeals from any baronial court and to protect any individual who sought his aid. These rules obviously weakened the power of the barons over their subjects and strengthened the king's position as the supreme judge and protector of the peace of the realm.

Philip III, the son of St. Louis, followed his father's policies as closely as he could, though he was a much less able ruler. Fortunately for the monarchy, a bureaucracy had been built up under St. Louis which was perfectly capable of carrying on the consolidation of royal power without much guidance from the king. Dynastic accidents also favored Philip. One of his uncles died without heirs and left the great county of Toulouse to the king; the heiress of Champagne married Philip's son and so brought another rich province into the royal domain. The only large fiefs not directly controlled by the king now lay isolated in the four corners of the realm—Flanders in the northeast, Brittany in the northwest, Aquitaine or Guienne (held by the king of England) in the southwest, and Burgundy in the southeast. Combinations of these four corner provinces were to make trouble in the fourteenth century but for the moment the king seemed in full control of France. Good government had given him the loyalty of his people; piety had strengthened the old alliance with the Church; a well-organized administration had dominated the feudal lords.

In the second half of the thirteenth century the king of France was certainly the most respected ruler of the West. No one else had the moral prestige which the kings of France had acquired. Five successive French kings had gone on Crusades, and the last three had died on Crusades—Louis VIII in the Albigensian Crusade, St. Louis in the Crusade against Tunis, Philip III in the unfortunate Crusade against Aragon in 1285. The French royal family had given the papacy steadfast support during the long quarrel with the Hohenstaufen. St. Louis had protected Innocent IV when he took refuge at Lyons; St. Louis' brother had conquered Manfred, the usurping king of Sicily; Philip III had tried to punish the king of Aragon for his attack on Sicily. In return, the popes had loaded the Capetian family with ecclesiastical privileges and had made it clear that they favored the growth of royal power in France.

Yet there were weaknesses in the position of the French king. One was in finance; as late as the death of Philip III in 1285 there were no general taxes paid by all subjects. The king depended on revenues from his lands, "gifts" (not always voluntary) from his towns, and grants from the Church. After 1285 taxation could no longer be avoided, but the absence of earlier precedents caused embarrassment to several generations of kings. The other weakness was one which we have already discussed—strong provincial feeling. It was still true that each new province added to the royal domain kept its laws and its basic institutions and that most of the king's subjects were more interested in the welfare of their province than in that of the realm. The king and the central government, working through the *baillis*, could keep this provincial loyalty from being dangerous to the crown, but they could not transform it into national civic spirit. Neither noble landholder nor wealthy merchant took much interest in the king's government, except when it infringed on local privileges. France was held together by the royal bureaucracy and was already beginning to show both the strengths and the weaknesses of a bureaucratic state.

England was different. Smaller, poorer, less populous than

France, it had the great advantage of national unity. The common law and the king's courts functioned in every part of the realm; provincial customs and institutions were unimportant. The strength of the Norman kings and the legal reforms of Henry II had forced all classes and all regions to participate in the work of government. In England, juries of freemen and knights of the shire performed many of the tasks which had to be done by bureaucrats in France. In thirteenth-century France the basic political fact was the steady growth of the royal domain and of royal power. In England it was the growth of political consciousness in members of the upper and middle classes.

The reign of John (1199–1216) set most of the problems with which English kings were to struggle for the rest of the century. John had more brains than character, more ambition than judgment. Suspicious and erratic, he never fully trusted his barons, and they, in turn, could never give him full loyalty. Yet John took on as adversaries two of the ablest rulers of the Middle Ages, Innocent III and Philip Augustus. As we have already seen, he was defeated in both contests. Innocent forced him to accept Stephen Langton as archbishop of Canterbury and Philip seized the larger part of his French possessions. Even if John had won, he might have had trouble with his barons. He had pushed his rights as feudal lord to the limit in order to raise money for his wars; he had punished vassals whom he distrusted without judgment of his court. Defeat made the barons angrier and bolder. Many of them had had lands in Normandy, now lost to Philip Augustus; most of them had been forced to give John large sums of money which had been wasted in unsuccessful wars. In 1215 a large group of barons rebelled, with the backing of the archbishop of Canterbury and the city of London. John had few active supporters; he was forced to accept their demands. On June 15 he agreed to the barons' terms and ordered the promulgation of the great charter which embodied them.

This great charter—Magna Carta—has become a landmark in

the history of English liberty. It is difficult for us to see it as it was when it was fresh and new, before it had acquired its halo of legend and symbolism. Yet the barons and churchmen who drafted it were not thinking in terms of parliaments and constitutions; they wanted to remedy specific grievances and to protect their own rights and privileges. The real difficulty is to see how a charter drawn up by a small aristocratic group to meet an immediate problem could become a symbol of liberty and constitutional government.

Magna Carta was a notable document, but it was not unique. All over Europe in the thirteenth and early fourteenth centuries the landholding classes, frightened by the steady growth of the power of central government, succeeded in obtaining charters which attempted to preserve their rights. The desire for precise legal definitions which would prevent quarrels and possible civil wars existed everywhere. But Magna Carta was the only one of these many charters which had a great future before it, which remained an important political document long after the Middle Ages had come to an end. It had two great qualities: it was national, not provincial; it imposed reasonable restraints on the central government without making it impossible for the central government to operate. The French charters of 1315 were long and detailed, but there was a separate charter for each great province and each province received different privileges. Later on it was easy for the French king to play one province off against another, or to claim that particular local privileges were harmful to the general welfare. The grants which Frederick II made to the ecclesiastical and secular princes of Germany were so extensive that they destroyed royal government. Each prince became practically a sovereign ruler, and when this stage was reached Frederick's charters had no further significance since they imposed no limitations on the princely governments, which were the only ones which really functioned in Germany. But England had been so thoroughly unified by the time of John that no one thought in

terms of local rights and privileges, and the barons showed remarkable restraint in imposing limitations on royal power. Some of this
restraint was probably due to the influence of Archbishop Langton,
who had no desire to see royal tyranny replaced by baronial
anarchy. It is also true that lesser barons and men of knightly rank
appreciated the protection given their holdings by royal courts
and would have opposed attempts to reduce this protection. But,
allowing full weight to these influences, the barons who drew up
the charter showed real political sense. They secured the maximum
concessions which were possible without doing serious damage to
the central government; they based even their most selfish demands
on principles which could be accepted by men of all classes. The
strong kings of the twelfth century had forced the barons to work
together, to take some responsibility for the general welfare, and
they could not forget this lesson, even in their moment of power.

"The king is and shall be below the law"—this was the significance of Magna Carta to one of the wisest English historians. This
idea was expressed with special clarity in two groups of articles,
those dealing with finance and those dealing with justice. In the
first part of the charter the barons forbade all the devices by which
John sought to make money out of feudal relationships. No large
sums could be collected without the consent of all the king's vassals,
given in a common council. Another important group of articles
demanded that the king, like his subjects, follow due process of
law in attempting to enforce his rights and redress his grievances.
No free man was to be imprisoned or punished except by the law
of the land. At the same time, the judicial reforms of Henry II were
not weakened; in fact, one article asked for more frequent use of
the procedures by which the king's courts monopolized all suits
dealing with real property. In short, Magna Carta made arbitrary
government difficult, but it did not make centralized government
impossible. As long as he followed the customs set forth in the
charter, the king had full control over the administration, and authority over all men in his realm.

And yet Magna Carta did mark an important shift in English politics. The barons had learned how to act as a group, how to pursue common interests instead of individual advantage. They were no longer thinking in terms of feudal separatism; they were beginning to see the possibility of controlling the central government for the benefit of their class. At the same time, they had learned how to make their demands seem more reasonable by basing them on legal principles and talk of the general welfare. The alternative to arbitrary royal government was no longer feudal anarchy; it was government limited by a baronial council. This made it possible for them to gain general support for their policies. No king after John could be sure that the propertied classes would support him instead of the aristocracy. During the century it became more and more necessary to consider and control public opinion in order to retain support for the royal government.

Magna Carta could not end the suspicion which existed between John and his barons. The barons made new demands and John secured papal absolution from his promises. A civil war began, but John died before either side could win a decisive victory. His son, Henry III (1216–1272), was too young to rule, and the Regent promptly confirmed the charter in order to conciliate the rebel barons. Henry added his own confirmation when he came of age, and Magna Carta was definitely accepted as part of the law of the land after this date, 1225. Even more important, the new political situation foreshadowed in Magna Carta became well-established during Henry's long reign. The king had to secure the approval of the barons for all major policy decisions and for all general taxes, and both king and barons began to realize the need for gaining the support of lesser landholders and business men. Out of this double necessity grew the English Parliament.

Henry might not have been so bound by the precedents established at the end of his father's reign if he had been a better politician. The barons could not oppose Henry because of his vices—unlike John, he was a virtuous, even a saintly monarch—

but they did doubt his judgment. He showed some real ability in administration; both Exchequer and law-courts made great advances during his reign. But he gave many important positions to relatives and friends who had little knowledge of English conditions. This aroused the jealousy of the English barons and weakened the government. Boniface of Savoy was a poor substitute for Stephen Langton as archbishop of Canterbury. At the same time, Henry made several expensive and futile efforts to regain some of the French lands lost by John. These unsuccessful expeditions not only diminished his prestige; they put him at the mercy of the barons, since he had to ask them for grants of taxes to finance his wars. Finally, Henry became involved in the papal struggle with the Hohenstaufen. He promised to pay for a war against Manfred in return for a grant of the Sicilian crown to his second son, Edmund. Henry never entirely fulfilled his promises, though he sent large sums to the pope, and in the end he lost both his money and the kingdom, which was given to Charles of Anjou.

This record of failure would have weakened any king, but it was especially dangerous in thirteenth-century England. As the unity of Latin Christendom weakened, national interests began to seem more important, and the English barons were clever enough to pose as the guardians of these interests. They could reproach Henry with his foreign favorites, with his interest in regaining French lands, with his involvement in the politics of distant Italy. They could claim to be the defenders of English liberties and English wealth against the whims of an internationally minded king. This line of attack would have had little meaning in the reign of Henry II, when king, barons, and clergy all had extensive interests in France. The fact that it was successful against Henry III shows how radically conditions had changed in less than a century.

The great weapon of the barons was their control of taxation. Magna Carta had sharply reduced the income derived from feudal relationships, and the king's other sources of revenue could barely support the government in time of peace. If he wanted to carry on an active policy he had to tax, and he could not tax without baronial consent. As the barons became convinced of Henry's unwisdom they made their grants smaller and smaller, and finally stopped them altogether. For over thirty years (1237–1269) Henry received no general tax from his people. This policy of obstruction naturally weakened the government and made Henry's plans seem even more impossible than they actually were. At the same time, it forced the king to call frequent meetings with his barons in order to try to overcome their opposition, and it was out of these meetings that Parliament finally emerged.

"Parliament" seems to have been something of a slang word at first; it was used to describe any occasion on which many men came together to talk about important affairs. By the 1240's it was being used in England to describe very full meetings of the king's court—meetings to which most of the great barons were summoned and at which the most important affairs of the realm were discussed. A Parliament was a plenary session of the king's court in every sense of the word. It had full judicial power; it could impose taxes; it could discuss policy and advise the king on appointments. Since it did such important work, its proceedings were watched with great interest and received the widest publicity possible under thirteenth-century conditions. English chronicles are full of accounts of the disputes which went on in Parliament between Henry III and his barons.

These impressive meetings of the king's court obviously offered opportunities to influence public opinion, or at least the opinion of the wealthier classes. The deadlock between king and barons made an appeal to these well-to-do groups desirable. Local government in England depended on the unpaid services of local notables, and no important policy could be carried out without their cooperation. Taxes were assessed and collected by well-to-do landholders in the counties and by leading merchants in the towns. Their opposition might reduce or slow up the collection of royal revenue; for example, the towns paid smaller sums to Henry III than they had to his grandfather, Henry II. Yet such men could not be easily coerced, especially when the central government was weakened by disagreement between king and barons. But if they were summoned to a meeting of the king's court, they would be bound by any decision reached there, and they might be persuaded, by the arguments of the great men who were present, to do their best to carry out the decision of the court.

The king and his ministers seem to have been the first to realize the possibility of using Parliament to secure the support of the men who controlled county and town governments. Early in his reign Henry III asked many shires to send knights to his court to discuss violations of Magna Carta. Perhaps in the 1240's, certainly in the 1250's, he again ordered the counties to send representative knights to meetings at which the defense of the realm and taxation were discussed. But Henry's opponents were not slow to take up the idea. When, in 1258, they became so exasperated with the king that they finally broke out in open rebellion, they too summoned knights of the shire to Parliaments which they controlled. And a little later the leader of the barons, Simon de Montfort (son of the Simon who defeated the Albigensians), went even further. In 1265, when many of his fellow-barons had deserted him, he tried to gain support from another class by summoning burgesses representing the towns, as well as knights representing the counties, to a Parliament.

The Barons' Rebellion (1258-1265) was not a success. For one thing, it was too polite a rebellion. Henry III was not executed, not even exiled; he remained nominally king but was supposed to govern through a Council dominated by the barons. Henry was free to build up a group of supporters and eventually to become strong enough to defeat Simon de Montfort in battle. Another weakness was the jealousy which many barons felt for their leader. Simon was English only on his mother's side, and the barons wanted government by committee, not government dominated by a man who was half a foreigner. Yet although the Barons' Rebellion failed, it marked another step in the growing political consciousness of the English upper and middle classes. The barons had shown that it was unwise for a king to follow policies which they disapproved; Henry attempted no new adventures during the remainder of his reign. Even more important, the king continued the plan of calling representatives of shires and boroughs to Parliament. The baronial government had done its best to gain the favor of these communities, and Henry found it necessary to follow their example. Knights and burgesses were summoned to his Parliament of 1268 and to the first assemblies which met in the reign of his son. The king was still the head of the government, but he had accepted the principle that he must explain and justify his actions to an assembly representing the upper and middle classes of his realm.

V. ECONOMIC, INTELLECTUAL, AND ARTISTIC ACTIVITIES IN THE THIRTEENTH CENTURY

During most of the thirteenth century, Western Europe enjoyed unprecedented peace and prosperity. A steady but moderate increase in prices stimulated production and trade. There were few prolonged wars except in Italy, and Italy was wealthy enough to recover quickly from the troubles of the papal-Hohenstaufen conflict. Italian shipping and banking expanded with amazing rapidity during the century and bound Western Europe together in a tight commercial network. The number of Italian ships, the size of individual ships, and the skill of Italian seamen increased with every decade; by the end of the century Italian fleets were sailing directly to England and Flanders. Overland routes were thronged with Italian pack-trains, and Italian business men were stationed in every important European town. The Italians had learned how to raise large sums of capital by combining their resources in partnerships or through loans; they had perfected banking techniques which put them far ahead of their competitors; and they very nearly monopolized the most profitable branches of

European trade. Almost all important exchange transactions, almost all large loans to popes, emperors, and kings, were made by Italian bankers.

The rest of Europe had not reached the Italian level of economic activity, but it was learning rapidly from the masters of business. The towns of southern France and the Aragonese port of Barcelona had a modest share of Mediterranean trade. English shipping was beginning to expand, thanks to the wine trade with Bordeaux and the wool trade with Flanders. Far more important was the growth of German shipping in the Baltic. The increase in population and the clearing of wooded land created a demand for grain, honey, furs, and timber from East Europe. These bulky cargoes were not as profitable as the silks and spices of the Orient, but they supported a large German merchant marine. German ships ranged from the Gulf of Finland to the Bay of Biscay; German merchants settled in large numbers in London and in Bruges; and the towns of north Germany grew in wealth and population.

Industry was less advanced than commerce. Yet the fine cloth of Flanders was sold everywhere in Europe, and even in the Islamic states of the Near East, while the metal wares of the Meuse valley had almost as wide a market. The hundreds of small towns scattered throughout Europe had assured local markets, for which they produced tools, and articles of clothing and ornamentation.

Agriculture was also reasonably prosperous, since both population and the standard of living were increasing. During the first half of the century, clearing new land was still a profitable investment and prices of agricultural products seem to have risen slowly until the 1280's. Free peasants, and those who had succeeded in commuting labor services into annual payments, were probably better off in the thirteenth century than they were to be again for generations. They were not greatly troubled by wars, and rising prices steadily decreased the real value of the fixed payments which they owed their lords. They were protected against new demands from their lords by the growing power of the secular state, and yet the state was not yet demanding much from them in the form of taxes or service. The peasants of north France probably profited most from this situation; there were more serfs in England, more wars in Italy, and more dangers from the unbridled power of great lords in Germany.

Prosperity alone does not guarantee great intellectual and artistic activity, but a certain surplus of manpower and resources is necessary before a society can devote much attention to enterprises which are not directly essential to its survival. Western Europe had such a surplus in the thirteenth century, and it had all the exciting new ideas of the twelfth century to stimulate its interest in scholarship, literature, and art. Certainly more young men were educated, more books were written, and more churches were built in the thirteenth than in any earlier medieval century.

The desire for knowledge and the demand for professional training, which had been striking features of the twelfth-century revival, became even more widespread after 1200. The older universities of Paris and Bologna continued to flourish, and new ones had to be founded to take care of the increasing number of students. Oxford became a real rival of Paris in philosophy, while Padua, Montpellier, and Orléans competed with Bologna in civil and canon law. The first Spanish universities also date from this period. Germany developed no university until the fourteenth century, but the Dominican school at Cologne, under the great scholar Albertus Magnus, was famous as a center of learning. University graduates, especially those with law degrees, continued to hold the highest posts in the Church and became prominent in the affairs of secular governments.

Just as important as the increase in the number of university students was the growth of interest in learning among men who had never attended universities. Most business men, many minor officials, and some landowners could read a little, and books were produced to satisfy their needs. Like other ages in which there has been a sudden increase in the reading population, the thirteenth

century saw a proliferation of handbooks and compendia—
what every man ought to know about theology or law in short
and readable form. Many of these books were written in the
vernacular; they ranged from encyclopedias, such as the *Livre
dou Tresor* of Brunetto Latini, to brief treatises on ethics and the
articles of the faith. Important historical works were also written
in the vernacular, especially on the subject of the Crusades. The
first great monument of French prose is Villehardouin's account
of the conquest of Constantinople; even more famous is Joinville's life of St. Louis, which is largely a description of the Sixth
Crusade. As these examples show, French was still the dominant
vernacular language; it was understood by nobles and townsmen
of all European countries. And the fact that prose masterpieces
could be written in French shows that the language had come of
age, for it is much harder to write good prose than good verse in
the early period of any language.

It was still true, however, that most serious writing was in Latin.
Here again, the audience was wider; there were many laymen who
could understand the relatively simple and straightforward Latin
of the thirteenth century. Treatises on the proper management of
great estates or digests of customary law were not written primarily for churchmen. University students, though technically
members of the clergy, often had a very secular point of view,
and many books were written by and for them. In fact, the
scholarly work of the thirteenth century cannot be separated into
the categories of secular and ecclesiastical learning; it influenced
all educated men.

Logic, order, and reason dominate the learning of the thirteenth century just as they dominate other activities. Each branch
of knowledge is arranged in a complete and orderly synthesis;
nothing is left out; no contradictions are permitted to remain.
The tendency toward encyclopedism, which we have already
noted in vernacular literature, was even stronger in Latin treatises.
For example, every important legal system was summarized in an

authoritative work. In England, Bracton wrote his great book on the common law, which brought logic and order into a rather empirical system and made it a worthy rival of the law of Rome. The unknown author of the *Summa de legibus* performed the same service for Norman law, and Accursius summarized and codified all the work of the commentators on Roman law. In other fields, Guillaume Durand wrote a definitive work on the significance of the ritual of the Church, and Jacopo da Voragine compiled an encyclopedia of legends of the saints.

The greatest and most lasting intellectual achievement of the thirteenth century was in the field of theology. Here its work has not been superseded; scholars are still discussing the ideas and praising the insights of men like Thomas Aquinas and Bonaventura. As in other fields, there was an urge to be encyclopedic, to discuss and summarize all previous work in theology. But the great scholars of the thirteenth century went far beyond this; they attempted to make a harmonious whole out of all the ideas and knowledge of their time. All doubtful problems were resolved; all conflicts between the new learning and the Christian faith were settled; everything was integrated into a complete philosophy of the relations of nature and of man with God. Such a feat could be attempted only in a period in which men felt sure that everything made sense, that there was a pattern in the universe which they could discern and explain.

The greatest of the medieval theologians was Thomas Aquinas, but it is well to remember that his *Summa Theologica* was based on the work of many other men. As a Dominican he profited from the scholarly activity of older members of his order and especially from the teaching of Albertus Magnus, who possessed almost as universal a mind as Thomas himself. Born in Italy, educated in Germany, a teacher at Paris, Thomas Aquinas knew the theologians and the schools of Western Europe. Yet his own genius took him beyond his predecessors and his contemporaries. The mere organization of his great book is an amazing achievement; every topic is clearly and logically related to the basic ideas of the faith. He does not have to labor to show how human concepts of law or of physics are related to religion; they enter naturally and inevitably into his discussion of theological problems. Granting his premises—the truths of the Christian faith and the basic principles of Aristotelian philosophy—his conclusions are coherent and convincing. His work has often been compared to that of the architects of the great medieval cathedrals, and there is some validity in the comparison, but no cathedral-builder reared such a vast structure out of such disparate materials.

The lawyers of the thirteenth century perfected legal systems which endured for centuries; the theologians left even more enduring monuments to their ability. There were no such striking achievements in other fields of thirteenth-century scholarship. Interest in the Latin classics continued to decline as students concentrated on logic, law, and theology. Medicine continued to attract students, but it acquired little new material and remained bound to the study of earlier texts. The great wave of translation of scientific and semi-scientific works from the eastern languages was spent by the third quarter of the thirteenth century; almost no new translations were made after that date. Medieval science still consisted largely in an effort to harmonize and to draw new conclusions from the authoritative works of Greek and Arab scholars. This was not always as easy as it had first seemed: the authorities were at times in conflict with each other or with Christian theology, and logic often gave results which seemed to be contradicted by common sense. Faced with these problems some scholars, notably the English bishop Robert Grosseteste, began to urge that conclusions drawn by logic be verified by experimental observation. Grosseteste's methods were continued at Oxford, and though experimentation never became dominant in medieval scientific study, enough was done to pave the way for the work of the early modern period.

Imaginative literature of the thirteenth century seems unimportant beside the great works of scholarship. This may be a warped view—students of literature find much of interest in the period—but some justification can be attempted for it. The remark would certainly be true for the eighteenth century—another intensely rational period—and perhaps for all centuries which seek order and reason above everything else. Certainly the originality and the verve of the twelfth century decrease after 1200. The old forms continue and are perfected. There are excellent versions of the *chansons de geste* and the Celtic legends, lyrics which are always technically skillful and occasionally touching, stories and legends which are still good reading. Yet the writers seem to have little new to say, and as the century goes on they seem to be satisfied either with technical perfection or with conveying information. Encyclopedism and the desire to teach creep into poetry. The great cycles of the *chansons de geste* are completed by mediocre poems which explain the ancestry or the missing years in the lives of heroes of earlier epics. The lyrics of the troubadours are full of the metaphysics of love and empty of real emotion; intricate rhyme-schemes and deliberately obscure language make them difficult for the ordinary reader to understand. In the latter part of the century, the most interesting lyrics are political—invectives against the pope, or the emperor, or the king of France—and political verse has seldom been great poetry.

The most popular poem of the thirteenth century—the *Roman de la Rose*—sums up many of these tendencies. It was begun as an allegory of love by Guillaume de Lorris in the 1230's: the lover seeks his beloved who is imprisoned in a fair garden. She is guarded by allegorical figures such as Danger and Jealousy; he is dissuaded by Reason, aided by Fair-Welcome, and so on. The allegory is a little over-elaborate for modern taste, but at its best it has some of the freshness and charm of the best early medieval poetry. Guillaume never finished the poem; it was completed a generation later by Jean de Meung. Jean almost loses sight of the allegory in his desire to convey information; his characters deliver long speeches which form a brief encyclopedia of thirteenth-century knowledge. The idealism of the earlier part of the poem vanishes; Jean is cynical and worldly-wise, especially on the subject of women. Yet medieval readers seemed untroubled by these discrepancies; all well-read men knew the poem and Chaucer, a century later, thought well enough of it to begin a translation into English.

Two other literary forms of the thirteenth century are important. Although some primitive dramatic compositions can be found earlier, the first fully developed medieval dramas come from the thirteenth century. Usually religious in content, they show that same desire for personifying abstract ideas or religious beliefs which we find in other writings of the period. Even more significant for understanding the contradictions in the society of the thirteenth century, are the *fabliaux*. These are short, satirical stories in verse, which exaggerate the real as much as allegory exaggerates the ideal. Their heroes are clever tricksters; their victims are the naïve and the stupid. All women in the *fabliaux* are lustful; all priests are gluttons or lechers; most representatives of public authority are corrupt. The peasant who makes a fool of his priest, the woman who makes a fool of her husband, and the priest who makes a fool of his bishop are glorified. It is never wise to ascribe too much importance to satire, which by definition must exaggerate, but these stories have only one moral—enjoy yourself as much as you can without being caught. They leave the impression that the leadership of the Church was weakening and that medieval idealism was wearing thin.

With all its weaknesses, the literature of the thirteenth century was read by and influenced later generations. Its basic forms were imitated by the second-raters and perfected by the great writers of the fourteenth and fifteenth centuries. Petrarch and Villon, Chaucer and Boccaccio used the forms and the plots of thirteenth-century lyrics and stories. Most of the great vernacular writers of the Renaissance drew from the same sources. Modern European literature has used much of this material; one of its main roots runs directly to this period of the Middle Ages.

The connection between art and literature was close in the thirteenth century, especially in sculpture and stained-glass work. Emile Mâle has shown that many scenes depicted in the cathedrals are simply illustrations of ideas and allegories discussed in the popular and didactic literature of the period. Architecture, naturally, was not so directly affected; there was, as yet, almost no theorizing on the subject. And yet, while architecture had its own life and its own tradition, deriving from the twelfth century, it had much in common with contemporary scholarship. The basic plan of the Gothic cathedral had been established earlier, but certain key relationships still had to be worked out. For example, how could the great, round rose windows of the façade be reconciled with the pointed arches of the interior? As Professor Panofsky has suggested, the architects of the thirteenth century had much the same problem as the theologians; they had to make a consistent and integrated pattern out of the varied ideas of their predecessors. That they succeeded shows both their technical ability and the quality of their artistic imagination.

A great cathedral of the thirteenth century is as logical as the Summa Theologica. It shows the bare ribs of its structure as confidently as Aquinas demonstrated his syllogisms; it resolves its architectural problems as surely as he did the contradictions among his authorities. It sums up the learning and the beliefs of the Western World in its windows and sculptures—history, allegory, legend, the Liberal Arts and the Labors of the Months, parables and dogmas, all are there. And yet, more than any other thirteenth-century activity, it escaped the coldness of intellectualism. The cathedrals are not only well planned; they are beautiful. The sculpture is not merely a visible demonstration of Christian truths; it has an esthetic as well as a rational appeal. The figures of Christ and the saints are idealized, and yet there is startling realism in some of the scenes of daily life. The allegorical figures are sometimes a little stiff and arid, but the Wise and Foolish Virgins are as alive on the portals of the cathedrals as they are in the text of the Gospels. The architects and sculptors of the cathedrals belong in the same company as the theologians and the lawyers of the thirteenth century—men who created systems so complete, so consistent, so satisfactory that their basic principles have endured for centuries.

5

The
Long
Autumn

THE PALACE OF THE POPES AT AVIGNON

I. THE CHANGING CLIMATE OF OPINION

WE CANNOT say that the Middle Ages ended with the thirteenth century—or with the sixteenth. Medieval civilization was full of vigor; it did not yield quickly or easily to new beliefs or new forms of organization. In one sense it never died, since many medieval ideas and institutions were slowly adapted to meet new conditions and survived well into the modern period. It is true, however, that from the end of the thirteenth century on, the climate of opinion became less favorable to medieval ways of thinking and acting. This change in the intellectual climate was like a change in the physical climate; it did not happen suddenly and the general trend was interrupted by temporary reversals. Medieval civilization declined through a long autumn period—an autumn which had its bright, sunny days as well as its frosts and rains. And the winter which followed the medieval autumn was short, and relatively mild, not like the terrible Fenris-winter which came at the end of the ancient world. The new climate was not entirely unlike the old; there was more continuity between late medieval and early modern civilization than between the civilization of the Roman Empire and that of the eighth century.

There is no doubt that the beginning of the change in the climate of opinion came in the last quarter of the thirteenth century. For once all the indices agree—there was a sharp break in politics and in economics, in thought and in the arts. Young men who witnessed the defeat of Manfred and the pious death of the crusading St. Louis were hardly more than middle-aged when Manfred's grandson reconquered Sicily from the papal champion, and St. Louis' grandson attacked a pope. Scholars who listened to the last lectures of Thomas Aquinas lived to hear his basic belief in the unity of all knowledge assailed. Sculptors who worked on the great cathedrals in the 1270's had to accept the change in fashion which substituted a pretty country girl with a baby for the majestic Virgin of the earlier period. Business men and land-owners saw mild prosperity and economic stability give place to stagnation and erratic fluctuations in the value of the currency.

We can recognize this change more easily than we can account for it. None of the obvious and naïve explanations of decline apply to this case. At the beginning of the slump there were no invasions, no great wars, no plagues, no wide-spread shortages of food or of raw materials. Some rural areas were overpopulated, but overpopulation had not yet caused any serious economic or medical problems. The decay was internal, not external—spiri-tual, not physical. It was connected with that growing interest in worldly knowledge, power, and wealth which had been so noticeable from the early years of the thirteenth century. The Church had combatted this tendency, especially through the mendicant orders, but the Church itself had become infected. It had concentrated on law and administration, on finance and politics; it had lost much of its prestige in the long war against the Hohenstaufen. The leadership of the Church had weakened just at a time when it needed to be strengthened. It would have been difficult in any case to apply the old ideals to the new prob-lems of an increasingly complex society; the task became impossible when the Church failed to realize the urgency of the problem. It is perhaps significant that no important new religious order was founded in the last medieval centuries. From the tenth century on, every new trend in secular society had been met and controlled by a new type of religious organization. But the fourteenth and fifteenth centuries produced no Cluny, no Franciscan Order; in fact, the officials of the Church rather frowned on new orders and suspected reforming leaders of dangerous radicalism.

As the leadership of the Church declined, due to its own weak-nesses and to the growing worldliness of the laity, medieval society was left without guidance. Christian ideals had not been repudiated, but they seemed remote and unclear; no one was sure just how they should be applied in specific situations. The authority of the Church had been weakened but no new authority had taken its place; religious leadership could neither be obeyed nor ignored. This situation created mental and moral instability; men swung wildly between gross sensualism and hysterical revivalism, or tried to make the best of both worlds by combining superstition with hypocrisy. The Church had been the symbol of cooperation and organization, and when that symbol was tarnished, the tasks of civilization became difficult. It was not easy to build up loyalty to a new symbol—the state—and until that loyalty was created Europe was confused and disorderly. We can see the same confusion and disorder today in developing societies in which the national state is replacing older faiths as the symbol of unity—and perhaps in other areas where the national state no longer seems a sufficient symbol.

II. THE FIRST FROSTS

The growing weakness of the Church was dramatically revealed in the pontificate of Boniface VIII (1294–1303). Boniface was an able canon lawyer, like most popes of the thirteenth century, and he had the canon lawyer's exalted opinion of papal authority. He failed to realize that no pope in 1300 could wield the authority of an Innocent III, and that the circumstances of his election had left him vulnerable to attack. The College of Cardinals had had serious differences on policy in the 1280's and found it impossible to agree on a new pope when Nicholas IV died in 1292. Finally, in 1294, they took the desperate step of electing a pious Italian hermit as Celestine V. Celestine was inexperienced, naïve, and completely bewildered by the political pressures to which he was subjected. After six months he resigned his office, and Boniface was chosen in his place. There was some doubt as to whether a canonically elected pope could resign, and grave suspicion that

Boniface had forced the resignation by underhanded means. Boniface became even more suspect when Celestine died in confinement shortly after his abdication. Boniface did not improve his position by quarreling with the powerful Roman family of the Colonna. The Colonna were probably to blame for beginning the fight, but Boniface reacted so violently that his opponents gained a good deal of sympathy. The two Colonna cardinals were deprived of their offices; a Crusade was preached against the family; their castles were destroyed and their lands devastated. But the Colonna in exile were more dangerous than the Colonna in Rome; they spread propaganda against the pope throughout Europe and encouraged secular leaders to oppose his authority.

Meanwhile, the powerful monarchies of England and France had drifted into war with each other. These countries were ruled by men who were very different from Henry III or St. Louis. Edward I and Philip IV were ambitious and determined to consolidate their power; they put the interests of their own kingdoms far ahead of those of the pope or of Christendom. Both kings had participated in unsuccessful Crusades which left them with poor opinions of papal policy. Both kings believed that no subject could be exempt from their authority and that they were justified in ignoring the privileges of the Church in order to defend their realms. Therefore, both Edward and Philip began to levy war taxes on their clergy in exactly the same way in which thirteenth-century popes had levied Crusade taxes.

The clergy of France and England made no serious protest over this action, since Crusade taxes had frequently been relinquished to secular rulers in order to aid papal policies. They were accustomed to giving money to their kings, and the Franco-English war seemed little more secular than the Crusades against Aragon or Sicily. Boniface, however, was indignant. Clerical taxation without papal consent deprived him of one of the main levers of political control and increased the independence of action of the Western kings. He therefore issued the bull *Clericis laicos*, forbidding any taxation of the clergy by lay rulers without his consent.

Edward and Philip were irritated by the prospective loss of revenue and put heavy pressure on the clergy to make them contribute in spite of the pope's order. This was to be expected; what was unexpected was that no one in England or France showed much enthusiasm for Boniface's position. There was no wave of indignation against the impious kings; instead, the clergy were accused of disloyalty and unwillingness to make sacrifices for the common welfare. The clergy themselves were so harassed by government officials and so worried by their unpopularity that they begged the pope to allow them to contribute to the taxes for defense. Left without any support, Boniface retreated, step by grudging step. In the end, he admitted that in an emergency kings could tax the clergy for defense without prior consultation with the pope. Since the kings could define both "emergency" and "defense," it was a substantial victory for them.

The fact that lay denunciations of the clergy proved more effective than papal denunciations of lay rulers should have warned Boniface that the climate was changing. The Church could no longer be sure of the basic loyalty of the people of Western Europe. Instead, loyalty was increasingly concentrated on secular governments. These governments had, on the whole, done a good job during the thirteenth century. They had maintained order and striven for justice; they had established patterns of obedience which were hard to break. The creation of strong central governments in both England and France had encouraged the emergence of the common interests which would eventually ripen into nationalism; already many men felt that the welfare of their kingdom was more important than the wishes of the pope. Short of heresy, these men would support their rulers in a struggle with the Church, and it was no longer as easy as it had been to convince them that disagreement with the Church in administrative or political disputes was the equivalent of heresy. In short, the

Church was losing one of its most important political weapons—the ability to stir up revolt against a disobedient king.

Boniface, however, did not yet realize his weakness. Some minor diplomatic victories restored his confidence, and in 1301 he became involved in a new dispute with King Philip of France. A French bishop was arrested on rather flimsy charges of treason; Boniface demanded his release and the king refused to comply. The issue could easily have been compromised—the bishop was released in the end without punishment—but both sides wanted a showdown. Boniface was determined to maintain the immunities of the clergy and the papal position as the final judge of all Christians. The French government was determined to assert its authority over all subjects and its complete independence of the pope in political matters.

In the propaganda war which followed, Boniface had decidedly the worst of it. His appeals to the clergy and people of France brought no response, whereas the French government organized impressive demonstrations against the pope. In 1302 a meeting of representatives of the clergy, nobility, and bourgeoisie—a precursor of the later Estates-General—was called to hear denunciations of Boniface, and during the next year charges against him were endorsed by local meetings held all over the country. The spontaneity of these demonstrations may well be doubted, but the fact remains that even the clergy could be threatened or cajoled into attacking Boniface, while no one could be persuaded to attack the king.

The climax came when the French government accused Boniface of heresy and misconduct, and ordered him to appear before a General Council of the Church. There was no precedent for such an action by a secular government, and the charges against the pope scarcely justified the extraordinary procedure. They ranged from the old grievances about Celestine and the Colonna to flimsy fabrications. For example, Boniface was accused of doubting the immortality of the soul because he had said that he would rather be a dog than a Frenchman—and a dog has no soul. But the charges were not important, while the technique was. Ecclesiastical weapons—the charge of heresy and the threat of a General Council—were being turned against the pope. The same methods which had been used to destroy Frederick II were being used to destroy Boniface VIII.

The final step in the French program was to arrest Boniface and hold him for trial by the Council. One of Philip's most trusted ministers, Guillaume de Nogaret, was sent to Italy in 1303 to accomplish this difficult task. Aided by the Colonna and other disgruntled Italians, he succeeded in capturing Boniface in his palace at Anagni. He kept the pope prisoner for three days; then the people of Anagni revolted and drove Nogaret from the town. But the shock had been too great for a man in his eighties; Boniface died soon after his release without taking any further steps against Philip and his minister.

If Boniface had failed to realize the strength of secular governments, the cardinals were more cautious. Their first choice, Benedict XI, did not make a direct attack on Philip, though he fulminated against Nogaret and his accomplices. When Benedict died after a brief pontificate, the cardinals retreated even further; they elected Clement V, a French archbishop who was not even a member of their College. Throughout his whole pontificate, Clement tried to avoid a conflict with Philip. Nogaret was absolved with only nominal penances (which were never accomplished) and Philip was praised for his "just and laudable zeal" in investigating the charges against Boniface. So ended the papacy of Gregory VII and Innocent III. The pope was still a great figure in European politics; he was consulted on most problems, and taxation of the clergy was easier if his consent were first obtained. But he could no longer initiate important policies; he could no longer command.

A perhaps fortuitous result of the pontificate of Clement V emphasized the decline in papal prestige. Clement, elected while he was in France, never went to Italy. He had good reasons: the absence of a central government allowed city quarrels and feuds among nobles to flourish, and the country must have seemed unsafe to a man accustomed to French order. But Clement was succeeded by another Frenchman, who also refused to go to Italy, and who fixed the papal residence at Avignon on the Rhone. Here the popes remained until 1377, and this "Babylonian Captivity" made Western Europeans even more critical of the central government of the Church. No one could think of Avignon as a holy city, and the absence of the halo of Rome emphasized weaknesses and concealed good qualities. The Avignonese popes were not willing to risk their lives, or even their comfort, to return to Rome, and in accepting the second best they lost much of their authority. They were not bad men, but they were primarily administrative and legal experts, not spiritual leaders. They ran the Church like a business organization, charging for their services, and underpaying their subordinates. These subordinates naturally recouped themselves by demanding fees and presents from men who had business at the papal court, and thus Avignon gained an unenviable reputation for bribery and injustice. Actually, it was no worse— probably somewhat better—than most secular courts, but this relative honesty had little appeal for men who were looking for a symbol to which they could give their loyalty. By the middle of the fourteenth century the papacy had lost most of its ability to guide and control Western civilization.

III. THE FAILURE OF THE SECULAR STATES

At the end of the thirteenth century there were indications that the sovereign state of the modern type was about to appear. The overlapping jurisdictions of the earlier period had been gradually eliminated; in most regions there was one dominant government which spoke with authority. In their struggle with Boniface, both Edward and Philip had claimed most of the attributes of sovereignty—complete independence of all outside powers, and the right to tax, judge, and legislate for all inhabitants of their realms. These claims had been made good in the conflict with the pope; even the clergy of France and England had loyally supported their kings and had accepted their decisions. Yet this movement toward a new type of political authority was checked just as it seemed to be acquiring irresistible momentum. During the fourteenth and early fifteenth centuries, secular governments were weakened by internal conflicts and foreign wars. The sovereign state was not fully established until the sixteenth century.

There were several reasons for dissatisfaction with secular governments. In the first place, over much of Europe the dominant governments did not control enough territory to satisfy all the aspirations of their subjects. It was difficult to give full loyalty to a small city-state in Italy or a petty principality in Germany, particularly when the chances were at least even that the city or the principality would, eventually, be merged with or conquered by a neighbor. Moreover, both "Germany" and "Italy" were something more than geographical expressions; they described real cultural and linguistic units. No one could forget that they once had been, and again might be, real instead of nominal kingdoms, and this prevented Germans and Italians from fully committing themselves to support of local governments. The Spanish kingdoms were more satisfactory foci of loyalty, but they were either imperfectly unified or harassed by disputed successions in the royal families. In the early fourteenth century England and France were the only states with all the attributes necessary for the emergence of sovereignty—size, unity, and firmly established dynasties.

The kings of France and England, however, made the same mistake which the popes had made a century earlier. They tried to move too fast, to gain their ends by questionable means. They preferred war to negotiation and legal chicanery to even-handed justice. They tried to manipulate public opinion instead of leading it; they relied on propaganda to cover their errors and their sins. These methods brought quick results—for a time—but in the end the governments were discredited, and subjects used the same unscrupulous means to attack their rulers. Only the early centralization, which had given people the habit of working together, the dogged efforts of the bureaucrats to keep the political machinery running, and the enormous reservoir of loyalty created by the good government of the thirteenth century prevented England and France from disintegrating in the late fourteenth and early fifteenth centuries.

The aims of the English and French kings were simple: to subordinate all privileged groups and areas in their states to royal authority, and to annex all the principalities on their borders which were too weak to defend themselves. The struggle over clerical taxation grew out of the first aim. The bullying of the clergy and the blackening of Boniface's character are typical of the methods which were used. The clergy was not the only group which was attacked; the nobility and the bourgeoisie were also forced to admit that their privileges could not protect them from royal demands. In both France and England recalcitrant towns and rebellious barons were punished by the imposition of ruinous fines or the confiscation of their property. These penalties were really a sort of blackmail; they were seldom enforced if the offender became fully obedient, but were promptly revived at the first signs of disobedience.

A notable example of the techniques of attacking a privileged group was the suppression of the Order of the Temple in France. Moslem conquest of the crusading states had deprived the Templars of their original excuse for existence, but they remained a wealthy and influential group. Their experience in transmitting funds to the East had introduced them to the trade of international banking and by the end of the thirteenth century they were treasurers for the king of France. Philip IV seems to have doubted their loyalty and he certainly coveted their wealth. In 1307 he suddenly ordered all the Templars arrested, and justified this flagrant violation of clerical privilege by charging them with heresy and immorality. Long imprisonment, repeated interrogations, and torture forced some of the Templars to confess their guilt, but investigations in other countries did not confirm the French charges. The pope, Clement V, was not convinced that the Order was guilty, but he followed his usual practice of appeasing the French king in order to avoid a scandal. The Order was suppressed by papal decree in 1312; its property was eventually turned over to the Order of the Hospital after the French government had paid itself well for its efforts to preserve the faith. Once again a secular government had been able to use the charge of heresy to destroy an opponent; even worse, the Church had been forced to allow its legal machinery to be used to cover an act of naked injustice.

The attack on privileged groups within the realm merged imperceptibly with the attack on weak neighbors. Overlapping political authority was just as natural under feudal conditions as it is unnatural in the modern state; the transition from the first to the second type of organization was bound to cause conflict. The concept of distinct boundaries, within which one ruler has supreme authority, was new at the end of the thirteenth century. In attempting to draw such boundaries, overlapping rights had to be ignored and tenuous claims of suzerainty exaggerated. Thus the French king clearly had some rights in the lands of the archbishop of Lyons, though the city itself was almost certainly in the Empire. When Philip took Lyons in 1310 he could argue that he was merely disciplining a rebellious vassal, though inhabitants of the Empire could protest that he was annexing imperial territory. In the same way, Edward I could use his claim to suzerainty over the Welsh princes as an excuse for conquering North Wales and subjecting it to English law. There was almost always some legal excuse for interfering with border principalities, and if it were exploited with sufficient lack of scruple it could easily lead to annexation.

There was always the danger, of course, that the prospective victims would not be impressed by lawyers' arguments and would resort to armed defense of their territories. The resistance of Welsh princes or imperial archbishops created no serious problems, but when Edward tried to annex Scotland while Philip sought to gain Flanders, both kings found that they had underestimated their opponents. The Scots and the Flemings resisted fiercely, and Edward and Philip found themselves involved in long and expensive wars, the first really serious wars which England or France had experienced for several generations. Neither war was successful; Scotland in the end remained entirely independent and Flanders saved most of its territory. A long war meant heavy taxation; an unsuccessful war meant that the taxation would be even more unpopular than usual. Both Edward and Philip in their later years found themselves in an awkward dilemma. If they taxed, they ran the risk of internal uprisings; if they failed to tax, their policy of conquest would collapse.

This situation increased the need for informing and influencing the opinions of the privileged classes. The need was there in any case; the attacks on clerical and aristocratic privileges, the strengthening of central government, the new concept of royal authority, all had to be explained and justified. But taxation touched the privileged classes on their sorest point; they were far more willing to surrender their political autonomy than their property. Heavy and repeated taxes simply could not be collected without the assent of the clergy, the nobility, and the bourgeoisie. Both Edward and Philip, therefore, had to devise means by which they could secure approval for, or at least acquiescence in, their policies.

Edward, of the two, had the easier task. England was already a political unit, and decisions made at the king's court were uniformly applied throughout the realm. Machinery for convoking representatives of the privileged classes in a central assembly was already available; the basic elements of the English Parliament had appeared in the last years of the reign of Henry III. All that

Edward had to do was to make regular and habitual a procedure which had earlier been used only on extraordinary occasions. In the first and peaceful part of his reign, Parliament remained primarily a high court of justice, composed of royal officials and a few prelates and barons. As his wars pressed more heavily upon him, Edward enlarged the membership of Parliament and used it more and more as a forum in which to explain his policies and to obtain consent to taxation. The knights, who represented the lesser landholders, were summoned regularly from the 1280's on. After 1295 the burgesses, who spoke for the towns, appeared at most of the sessions in which taxation was discussed and were sometimes called even when no taxes were requested. By Edward's death in 1307, a full session of Parliament was expected to include these groups of representatives as well as bishops, earls, and barons.

In making Parliament an essential element in the work of the English government, Edward had no idea of surrendering any of his power. English custom already forbade taxation without consent; it was more efficient to obtain that consent in a single meeting with representatives of all important classes in English society than to negotiate separately with individual barons and communities. As for policy, Edward always kept the initiative. He explained what he was going to do and why; he did not invite suggestions or criticisms. A great lord might perhaps protest, but a knight or burgess could do nothing but listen. Edward clearly thought of Parliament as a device for gaining the maximum amount of publicity and support for his actions with the minimum amount of trouble. By claiming that Parliament represented the community of the realm he gained a strong legal and moral position; by explaining his policies to it he was able to influence the opinions of the privileged classes. But none of these actions gave Parliament an independent position; he controlled it just as he did all other organs of government.

Yet Edward had placed Parliament in a position which made it dangerous to his weaker successors. It had great authority and prestige because it was the place where the king and his ministers met with the leading men of the country. It was the highest court of justice and could reverse the judgments of lower courts and settle doubtful questions of law. As the great council of the kingdom it could advise the ruler on any problem he laid before it. It represented the community of the realm and could therefore assent to departures from established custom, such as new laws and taxes. A strong king saved time and trouble by this concentration of functions in one body, but this very concentration also offered an opportunity to the baronial opposition. A session of Parliament brought together all the great men of England; they could discuss their grievances and plan their protests. And, since so many important acts of government were habitually given their final sanction in Parliament, the barons might hope to gain control of the government by gaining control of Parliament.

In France, it was more difficult to influence the opinion of the upper classes. Provincial loyalties were still strong, and there were no precedents for a central assembly of representatives of the realm. The great barons of France had not acquired the habit of working together at the king's court; the only men who thought in terms of the kingdom as a whole were the bureaucrats, who were devoted servants of the king. And yet Philip IV needed public support even more than Edward. His attack on the Church was pushed further; his taxes were more varied and more unprecedented. He tried the expedient of a general assembly on three occasions—in 1302 to justify his attack on Boniface, in 1308 to explain his action against the Temple, and in 1314 to gain support for a tax for the Flemish war. But these assemblies of clergymen, nobles, and townsmen were far less frequent and far less effective than meetings of the English Parliament. The French assemblies had little prestige and little authority; unlike the English Parliament, they did not grow out of the great council or the high court. They were obviously convened purely for purposes of propaganda; they could not make decisions which were legally binding on the whole kingdom. Philip realized this; he never dared to collect a tax solely on the authority of a grant by the estates of the realm. To obtain effective consent to taxation and support for his policies he had to use the laborious and time-consuming procedure of sending agents all through France to talk to individual barons and local assemblies. These agents were more successful in obtaining support for Philip's policies than in raising money for his wars. Local communities did not hesitate to associate themselves with the attack on Boniface, but they put many limitations on their grants of taxes. French taxes produced little more than English, though the population of France was four or five times greater. Yet in the long run, Philip's system was safer than Edward's. The Estates-General that grew out of Philip's assemblies were never a successful rallying-point for opposition to the king, and the main organs of government never escaped from the control of the king and the bureaucracy.

The ingenuity displayed by both Edward and Philip in controlling public opinion could not avert the consequences of premature and tactless assertion of the principle of sovereign authority. The death of both kings was followed by aristocratic rebellions. Neither rebellion was very successful: the French king confirmed provincial liberties in a series of charters which, if narrowly interpreted, put little restraint on royal authority; the English king assented to ordinances limiting his power which were later repealed. But the barons were more encouraged by their initial successes than discouraged by their failures, and they kept up their pressure on the royal governments of both kingdoms. They had discovered that support for strong monarchy was less intense and less effective than it had been in the thirteenth century. They had found that they could pose as guardians of legality and protectors of property rights against kings who perverted justice and multiplied taxes. Not everyone believed the barons when they claimed to be disinterested upholders of righteousness, but the kings were vulnerable in many ways. The deposition of Edward II in 1327, and arguments about the succession to the throne in France meant that in both countries the kings needed the support of the aristocracy. The tax system was unfair, inefficient, and seldom produced enough money for the needs of the government. As a result of these weaknesses, the barons were often able to neutralize the old tendency of the people to rally to the side of the king in any dispute between him and the aristocracy.

Deprived of the whole-hearted support of their people, the kings of France and England had to compromise with their barons. They had to give them a greater place in their governments; they had to pay them with lands and with pensions in order to retain their loyalty. They had to rely on them for military support; the armies of France and England were composed of companies raised by the barons and paid by the barons out of their grants from the royal treasuries. These companies were often more loyal to their commanders than to the king; they could be used for rebellions and civil wars. As a result, the fourteenth and fifteenth centuries saw the development of what has been called "bastard feudalism" in both England and France.

The appropriateness of this term is questionable because the nobles, for the most part, did not want to split their kingdoms into semi-independent principalities; they wanted to control the central governments in order to gain wealth and power. As a result, stable and efficient administration became almost impossible. The barons could not work together on any constructive plans, and they were as jealous of leaders from their own ranks as they were of their kings. Politics fell into a dismal pattern of baronial revolt, quarrels among the successful rebels, alliance between the king and a baronial faction, temporary revival of royal authority, and a new baronial revolt. Of the nine kings of England who ruled between 1307 and 1485, six were deposed. The kings of France were more successful in keeping their thrones, but they very nearly lost their country. Dukes and counts intrigued and waged war on each other in order to gain grants of land and revenues. The most dangerous of these great lords were the dukes of Burgundy, who had added the Low Countries to their original holdings in southeast France. In order to strengthen their position and weaken their enemies, they first tried to transfer the French crown to the king of England, and then sought to set up an independent kingdom of their own.

Political instability was made worse by the Hundred Years' War, which was waged intermittently from 1337 to 1453. There were many excuses for war between England and France—trade quarrels, the old irritant of English possession of Gascony, attempts to place the Low Countries in either the French or English sphere of influence—but these excuses had existed earlier without provoking so serious a conflict. The real reason for the long war was that neither kings nor barons had a policy or strong support in their own country. They were therefore inclined to postpone the solution of domestic problems and seek popularity through military adventures.

The war dragged on for generations before either side won a permanent victory. The English almost ended French resistance on two occasions: once under Edward III after the battles of Crécy (1346) and Poitiers (1356); once under Henry V after Agincourt (1415). Each time the French rallied under a great leader—Du Guesclin in the fourteenth century and Joan of Arc in the fifteenth—and drove the English back. Each country suffered severely from the conflict. The English were demoralized by their repeated failure to hold their conquests. Each period of defeat abroad was followed by revolution or civil war at home. The French, like the English, suffered from internal conflicts and in addition had large parts of their country devastated by military campaigns. On the other hand, the fact that the French, in the end, were victorious gave them a psychological advantage. Charles VII, who had given Joan of Arc rather grudging support, emerged as Charles the Victorious and regained some of the prestige which the monarchy had lost in the last century and a half.

As a result, the restoration of royal authority in France was well advanced by 1450, more than a generation before a similar revival took place in England. The failure in France touched off the Wars of the Roses in England. Ostensibly, these wars were waged to determine which branch of the royal family had the better right to the throne. Actually, they were struggles between baronial factions to gain land and profitable offices. The Wars of the Roses kept England weak and divided during the third quarter of the fifteenth century. Only when the Tudors came to the throne in 1485 was England able to follow the French example and re-establish strong monarchy.

IV. LOST IN THE FOG

The failure of both religious and secular leadership intensified the impact of difficulties which would have been hard to meet in any case. As we have already seen, the economy of Western Europe was slowing down in the last decade of the thirteenth century, and a serious depression began soon after 1300. This depression, one of the worst in history, persisted throughout the fourteenth, and well into the fifteenth centuries. Population was stagnant or declining; there were no new markets and no significant additions to the labor force. Production was not increasing and what surpluses did exist were consumed in futile and prolonged wars. The real prices of many commodities declined and many producers found it difficult to make a profit. Most governments became bankrupt, and their financial collapse ruined many of the old banking companies which had provided credit for international commerce. In attempting to raise money for their wars, European rulers regularly inflated their currencies. In the long run, this may have helped to counteract the depressing effects of declining prices, but the operation was usually performed so clumsily that it caused violent swings in prices and loss of confidence on the part of business men.

In these circumstances, it is not surprising that men sought to preserve what they had rather than to enlarge their incomes by new ventures. This attitude was reflected in legislation and guild regulations. Maximum wages were proclaimed, so that agricultural laborers would not deprive landowners of their profits. Guilds were allowed to establish monopolies, and to limit the number of men entering a trade, so that every master workman would have his fair share of a static market. In short, an attempt was made to revive the old status economy, in which a man's economic situation was determined by the accident of birth. The increased power of the aristocracy was both a cause and a result of this tendency.

But the status economy of the early Middle Ages had been based on a social organization in which almost everyone had some land and in which money income was unimportant. By the fourteenth century there were thousands of landless men in every region of Western Europe, and even those with land depended on money incomes. Unemployment was a real problem in great industrial centers such as the Flemish weaving towns, while low wages created discontent in agricultural areas. The upper classes could manipulate economic regulations to their advantage, or evade them altogether. Landholding peasants profited from inflation and a shortage of farmers with enough capital to lease land. Such peasants could obtain good land at relatively low rents, and thus became moderately prosperous. For the same reasons, merchants and artisans with sufficient skill and capital were able to maintain a comfortable level of living. But poor artisans and industrial and agricultural laborers lived in misery and could find no peaceful way of bettering their condition. As a result, there was a long series of rebellions in the fourteenth and fifteenth centuries. In Italy and in Flanders the urban proletariat was the chief element; in England, France, and Germany the peasants played a larger rôle, though they were supported by discontented elements in the towns. These rebellions were uniformly unsuccessful; peasants and artisans did not have the equipment, the experience, or the organization necessary for sustained military action. The fact that they revolted in the face of these handicaps shows how bad their economic situation was.

These social and economic problems were made worse by the great disaster of the Black Death. This outbreak of the bubonic plague reached the Mediterranean in the 1340's and swept in a great arc through Western Europe, reaching its peak about the middle of the century. Lesser outbreaks continued for the next fifty years. In the absence of any trustworthy vital statistics it is impossible to estimate the mortality; the few figures we have come from the towns, which were harder hit than the open country. Some crowded communities may have lost 30 to 40 per cent of their inhabitants, though the overall rate was certainly lower. But even if we assume a death-rate of only 20 per cent, the physical and moral impact of the disease was terrific. No modern war has caused such losses, yet the death-rate of the First World War shook the foundations of our society. And the Black Death was worse than war, since nothing could be done to resist its attack. Medical knowledge was hopelessly inadequate; there was no one to recommend even the most rudimentary sanitary precautions. Men either waited hopelessly for the onset of a foul, agonizing disease, or abandoned all their responsibilities and fled to uninfected areas. The best men were most certain to die—officials who tried to preserve order in the hysterical towns, doctors and priests who remained to console the dying, scholars who continued their studies. The survivors, deprived of many of their natural leaders, were shaken and unstable for decades after the peak years of the great plague.

The economic consequences of the Black Death were also serious. For at least a generation population declined, with disastrous effects on an economy which had already become stagnant. Quarrels broke out among the propertied classes over division of dwindling income; landlords joined in civil wars and merchants and bankers took part in urban uprisings. At the same time, labor-

ers tried to take advantage of the manpower shortage to demand
increased wages. In the absence of increased production, this
would have meant decreased incomes for the upper classes, and
they naturally reacted by freezing wages at a low level. This legislation was sometimes evaded, but it was enforced strictly enough
to cause violent protests. The most dangerous rebellions of the
lower classes came in the half-century after the Black Death. Only
in the fifteenth century were the economic consequences of the
plague finally overcome.

By that time, Western Europe had suffered another shock to its
confidence—the Great Schism in the Church. The Avignonese
popes had always had a feeling of guilt about their absence from
Rome, and in 1377 Gregory XI returned to the Holy City. He
died there one year later, and the cardinals, under considerable
pressure from the Roman populace, elected the Italian Urban
VI as his successor. Many of the cardinals were Frenchmen, and
they soon found both Italy and the new pope too violent for
their comfort. After Urban had imprisoned some of them, most of
the remaining cardinals fled to Avignon. They claimed that the
election of Urban had been invalid, because they had been threatened by the Roman mob, and proceeded to elect a new pope,
Clement VII. They did not convince everyone, but they did succeed in gaining the support of many theologians and secular rulers.
For the first time since the disputed election of Innocent II in
1130 there was real doubt as to who was the rightful pope. Even
worse, the doubt continued for over forty years, as two groups
of cardinals continued to elect rival popes.

Secular rulers naturally supported the pope whom they thought
favorable to their interests. Thus the king of France backed the
Avignonese pope, whereas the king of England adhered to the
Roman claimant. Scotland, the ancient ally of France, and the
Spanish kingdoms were on the Avignonese side; Germany, as
usual, was divided; the Italian states supported Rome. Less worldly
people were sincerely distressed, and put forth a series of sug-

gestions for healing the breach in the Church. The solution which received the greatest support called for a General Council to settle the issue, but neither pope liked this idea. A General Council which chose a pope might claim to be superior to the pope. Moreover, many of the supporters of a General Council were also reformers, and some of their ideas seemed to threaten the administration and financial system of the Church.

In spite of this opposition, a General Council met at Pisa in 1409. It did little for reform and made the Schism worse by denouncing both the Roman and Avignonese claimants and electing a third pope. Since the Pisan candidate was not accepted by most Catholics, the situation became so ridiculous that even secular rulers felt that something had to be done. A new Council met at Constance from 1414 to 1418, under strong pressure from the peoples and governments of Europe. It was, in a way, the first of the great European international congresses, a precursor of Vienna and Versailles. Though the clergy theoretically controlled the Council, the final outcome depended on the agreement of kings and princes. The Avignonese and Pisan popes were deposed; the Roman pope resigned, and a new pope was chosen who was generally recognized.

The Schism was healed, but the scars remained. The new line of popes first devoted themselves to wiping out the theory of conciliar supremacy. They had no desire to see papal absolutism turned into a parliamentary monarchy. They had also been shocked by the degree to which secular rulers had influenced the delegations from their countries at Constance. They won their fight to reestablish papal authority, but this left them no energy for their other tasks. They paid no attention to the demands for reform which were increasing in intensity; they did not even maintain their interest in European politics. By the second half of the fifteenth century the papal monarchy had become an Italian principality. The popes spent most of their time in defending the States of the Church, providing fortunes for their relatives, and posing as patrons of literature and art. They had had an opportunity to re-establish their leadership in the burst of jubilation which greeted the end of the Great Schism. They missed this chance; they were not to have another before the Reformation.

The great majority of the people of Europe had retained their faith through all the physical and spiritual sufferings caused by war, plague, and schism. But they had been badly shaken by these experiences, and the failure of the Church to give them any clear guidance increased their instability. The violence of their lives was reflected in the violent swings of their religious behavior. They oscillated between the extremes of superstition and blasphemy; they tried to atone for their failure to practice Christianity by multiplying ceremonies and special devotions to the saints. Superstitious practices, denounced by both Catholics and Protestants in the next century, flourished as never before. The witchcraft delusion, which had scarcely been known in the thirteenth century, reached its peak in the fifteenth, but it is important to note that it was a double delusion. Not all the accused were innocent victims of ignorant zealots; there were men and women who deliberately strove to gain worldly advantages by worshipping the powers of evil. There was a cult of Satanism; there were sacrifices, even human sacrifices, to evil spirits; there were people who believed that they had gained supernatural powers by selling their souls to the devil. Everyone accepted the possibility of black magic, so it was easy for religious demagogues to stir up a wave of persecution which engulfed both the guilty and the innocent.

Behind all this turmoil, one fact stands out. The people of Western Europe were still seeking personal experience in religion and most of them were not gaining it through the conventional ministrations of the Church. This dissatisfaction was expressed in revivalism and popular superstition, but an even more significant manifestation was the growth of mystical and heretical sects. The fourteenth and fifteenth centuries were a great period of mysticism, because the mystics stressed the importance of the individual's relationship with God, and minimized the problems of Church organization. The mystics had great influence not only on their own age but on subsequent generations; Luther found many of his ideas foreshadowed in their works. These mystics were occasionally criticized for over-emphasizing individual experience and underestimating the efficacy of the Church's sacramental system, but most of them remained within the bounds of orthodoxy.

Other reformers, though influenced by the ideas of the mystics, concentrated their attacks on the organization and administration of the Church. They believed that wealth and over-centralization produced corruption and indifference to religious duties among the clergy, and that laymen in turn were led astray by evil shepherds. They urged that the Church be deprived of all or some of its wealth and that it be subjected, in some degree, to the control of laymen. These attacks were bitterly resented by the hierarchy and the men who made them were denounced as heretics. But the reformers had many supporters, and the Church never succeeded in ending all criticisms.

The two most influential reformers were John Wycliffe of England (1327–1384) and John Huss of Bohemia (1369–1415). Wycliffe went beyond ordinary reformers by attacking not merely the abuse of clerical privileges, but the theories on which the privileges were based. He argued that every individual was directly responsible to God, and that the organized Church was not absolutely necessary for salvation. Secular rulers, in his view, would probably be better administrators of property devoted to religious purposes than the clergy. To diminish the importance of the clergy, Wycliffe attacked the sacramental system, and particularly the idea that in the Mass the bread and wine were changed into the body and blood of Christ. Huss had independently developed similar ideas, and knowledge of Wycliffe's work strengthened his convictions. As a symbol of the increased importance of the laity, Huss insisted that they be allowed to receive the cup as well as the consecrated wafer at communion.

Wycliffe was forced out of his Oxford professorship, but was allowed to retire to a country parish where he died peacefully in 1384. His followers, the Lollards, were less fortunate. They were accused of causing rebellions among the lower classes, and this cost them the support of the aristocracy, who at first had been attracted by the argument that laymen should control Church property. Lollard leaders were executed, and the heresy was practically wiped out. The one important survival was a Lollard translation of the Bible, which influenced English reformers of the sixteenth century.

The Hussites suffered as greatly as the Lollards, but were more successful in surviving. Huss was able to identify his cause with Czech national feeling, and orthodoxy with the Germans, who were gaining political control of Bohemia. As a result, he probably had a majority of the Czech population of Bohemia on his side. Huss and several of his most important supporters were executed; Crusades were preached against the sect, and Bohemia was repeatedly invaded by German armies, but the Catholics never won a complete victory. Some of the Hussites made a compromise with the pope, by which they were allowed to retain certain privileges, notably the use of the communion cup by the laity. Hussite churches survived to the time of the Reformation, when Luther discovered that many of his doctrines could be supported by references to the works of John Huss.

V. PREMATURE SPRING IN ITALY

Italy escaped some of the more disturbing effects of the decline of medieval civilization. This was due, in part, to the fact that neither war nor economic depression affected Italy as seriously as the northern countries. There were many little wars in Italy, but no major conflict, and it is unlikely that the Italians ever devoted as large a proportion of their income to war as did the inhabitants of France and England. Moreover, Italy maintained its economic vitality in spite of general stagnation in the rest of Europe. Bankers who had lent money to the northern kings were ruined when these rulers repudiated their obligations, but Italians retained their near-monopoly of international banking and discovered new ways to make money out of their operations. The most profitable branches of international trade also remained firmly in Italian hands; in fact, the Italians probably increased their share of Mediterranean trade during the fourteenth century. The Italians also increased their share in European luxury production; for example, they supplanted Flanders as the source of the finest cloth, even though they had to import almost all their wool. Thus Italian cities continued to grow in wealth and population at a time when northern towns did well to hold their own.

Even more important, the Italians were not greatly shocked by the decay of medieval institutions and the tarnishing of medieval ideals. Italy, with its strong classical heritage, had never been fully committed to the medieval way of life and its passing was not regretted. The Italians had never been well governed, so the failure of fourteenth-century rulers did not perturb them. The Italians had been too close to the center of ecclesiastical power to have any illusions about the papacy, so the worldliness of four-teenth-century prelates did not scandalize them. The thirteenth century, to the transalpine peoples, was a Golden Age which they strove to recapture. To the Italians, it was a period of oppression by Church and Empire from which they were glad to escape. The near anarchy of the fourteenth century, which horrified the North, was the liberty for which the Italians had been striving. There-fore, more than any other people, they accepted the new conditions of life without regret. With no feeling of guilt, their individual-ism could expand outward into secular activities, rather than turning inward toward religious contemplation, as was the case with many northerners.

The change in attitudes is illustrated by the work of three great Italian writers: Dante, Petrarch, and Boccaccio. Dante (1265–

1321) belonged to the Christian Commonwealth of the thirteenth century rather than to Italy of the Renaissance. He believed that the Empire was as necessary for human welfare as the Church for human salvation, and that the two powers should work together on their God-given tasks. His great poem, the *Divine Comedy*, was an exposition of Christian theology; parts of it (especially the Paradise) are Thomas Aquinas put into verse. But there was more to the *Divine Comedy* than theology; it was a matchless commentary on human life. This was especially true of the first section of the poem, the Inferno, with its unsurpassed portraits of individuals. Moreover, the Inferno was the part of the poem which made the greatest impression on Italian thought, and Dante's guide through Hell was Vergil. Vergil, to Dante, was a symbol of human reason, but to the Italians he was also a symbol of the superiority of classical learning. Dante's political theories were anachronistic even in his day, and his devotion to them was one reason why he died in exile. It was his skill as a poet, his knowledge as a scholar, and his appreciation of the classics which made him a precursor of the Renaissance.

Petrarch (1304–1374) did not have Dante's firm moral convictions, and vacillated all his life between his desire for human fame and his fear that this vanity might endanger his soul. Unlike Dante, who accepted all learning as equally valuable, Petrarch rejected medieval scholarship. He felt that classical authors were far superior in style and reasoning power to their medieval successors, and condemned almost everything written after the fall of Rome as barbarous. He insisted that the poet and scholar should be honored by all other men, and his own claim to eminence was accepted by most of his contemporaries. More than any other man, he established the cult of classical scholarship in Italy. His letters reveal his vanity and his uneasy conscience, but also his real devotion to literature. And his Italian verses show that underneath the pomposity and pedantry there was a real poet.

Boccaccio (1313–1375) marks the end of the cycle. Dante's

religious beliefs overrode all worldly considerations; Petrarch wanted success in this world at least as much as salvation in the next; Boccaccio sought worldly enjoyment first and thought of religion only when he was badly frightened. Like Petrarch, he was an earnest student of the classics, but his popular writings proved far more enduring than his scholarly work. His most famous book, the *Decameron*, is essentially a collection of *fabliaux*, placed in an elegant setting and told in a polished style. Boccaccio revered Dante as an accomplished poet, but he was almost unable to understand Dante's moral convictions or his love of symbolism and allegory.

By the time of Boccaccio's death, the interests he typified were becoming dominant among the prosperous inhabitants of the Italian towns. Men wanted to enjoy life, not in a crude or vulgar way, but with elegance and style. Life was to be a work of art; luxury was to be restrained by good taste, and the rich and powerful were to justify their position by patronizing artists and scholars. *Virtù*—manliness—became the most highly praised quality. The individual was to express himself fully and boldly—a magnificent vice was better than a humdrum virtue. The Italians thought that they had found a model for their secular, individualistic society in ancient Rome and therefore the classics became the standard by which every activity was tested. Actually, the Italians imitated Rome much less than they claimed, and some of their greatest achievements (for example, their painting) owed little to classical models. On the other hand, while they condemned the ignorance and superstition of the Middle Ages, they relied much more than they would admit on medieval technology, scholarship, and institutions.

Yet attitudes changed even when techniques were preserved. The Italians accepted, at least in principle, the leadership of the Church, and the idea that all human values were derived from the eternal law of God. Nevertheless, they followed leaders who glorified life in this world—the artists who idealized the human body, the scholars who extolled the power of the human mind, the princes who proclaimed the primacy of the secular state. Released from old restraints, sure of the value of their new insights, they put tremendous energy into all their activities. Their accomplishments were first envied, then imitated by Europeans living beyond the Alps, and thus the ideas and techniques of the Italian Renaissance became part of the common Western tradition.

In scholarship, the Italians used almost all the Latin materials which had survived the fall of Rome, and which had been neglected when medieval scholars, after 1200, became more interested in their own problems. Because they were concerned with style, the Italians prepared better texts of these classical works than the Middle Ages had ever known. Even more important, in the fifteenth century there was a great wave of enthusiasm in Italy for the study of Greek. Greek scientific and logical texts had been translated into Latin in the twelfth and thirteenth centuries, but Greek literature had been neglected, and few Westerners had ever made a thorough study of the language. The Italians of the Renaissance remedied these deficiencies and so the Greek literary tradition—far more original and stimulating than the Latin—began to have a direct impact on Western thought. Through the Italian example, study of the Latin and Greek classics became for three centuries the basis of all higher education in Western Europe.

In focusing on literature, the Italians tended to neglect the study of natural science. The neglect was not absolute, due to the fact that the old medieval curriculum, based on Aristotle's scientific and logical works, existed side by side with the new classical curriculum in Italian universities. At Padua, especially, there were able professors of mathematics and physics, though there were transalpine scholars who were at least their equals. The one field in which Italians were pre-eminent was anatomy, thanks to the combination of the old scholastic study of medicine with the new interest of artists in accurately depicting the human body. Thus Vesalius, in 1543, published a work on anatomy which superseded all earlier studies. On the other hand, Leonardo da Vinci, who had the most original ideas about science of any Italian, never pushed any of his studies beyond casual jottings in a notebook. The Italian climate of opinion encouraged art rather than science, so Leonardo devoted most of his great ability to painting and sculpture.

Nevertheless, there was an important scientific element in the literary scholarship of the Italians. As they prepared grammars and dictionaries, or established more accurate texts of classical works, they had to use techniques which were essentially scientific. They collected scattered facts and arranged them in meaningful categories; they formulated hypotheses about etymologies, and established general laws of grammar. Thus they helped to create attitudes which eventually favored the development of natural science. Moreover, in studying the history of the ancient world, they had to insist on their right to free investigation, even when it led them into conflict with established tradition. For example, Lorenzo Valla demonstrated by textual criticism that the Donation of Constantine, one of the basic documents in the papal claim to temporal supremacy in the West, was a forgery.

In art, even more than in scholarship, the Italians developed styles and techniques which were widely different from those of the twelfth and thirteenth centuries. Medieval artists were not interested primarily in realism, although some of their decorative figures were extraordinarily lifelike. Their principal interest was in telling a story or expressing an idea; symbolism was more efficient and more effective in accomplishing these aims. The Italians set themselves the task of reproducing the human figure as accurately as possible, of detaching it from its background and making it a separate, recognizable individual. The greatest of them went beyond this and idealized their individuals until they became demi-gods. But it was usually human beauty, human wisdom, human virtue that were idealized, not religious concepts or abstract intellectual qualities.

In achieving these results, the Italians had to solve a host of technical problems. They worked out the principles of perspec-

tive; they solved problems of lighting; they studied anatomy endlessly and patiently. Sculptors had to learn the art of casting metal;
painters had to learn how to work with oil colors (one of the few
techniques imported from the North). For over two hundred years
there was active experimentation, which makes this one of the
most interesting periods in the history of art. The first great
innovator, Giotto, was a contemporary of Dante; the brilliant
experimentalists like Masaccio and Mantegna lived in the period
of the great revival of classical studies; the masters who summed
up all the work of their predecessors—Michelangelo, Leonardo da
Vinci, and Raphael—were active in the early sixteenth century. At
that point, the Italians began to lose their leadership in art. They
were satisfied with the style which they had perfected, and for
half a century they imitated it and weakened it. Meanwhile their
former pupils of the transalpine countries found new problems,
and in solving them created new styles which superseded the
Italian models.

Italy also developed a new type of statecraft. The collapse of
the Empire and the retreat of the papacy to Avignon had removed
the poles around which federations of towns and princes had
coalesced. Left to its own devices, Italy north of Naples split into
dozens of principalities and city-states. The weaker units were
annexed by stronger neighbors, but no one state was able to dominate the whole peninsula. At the same time, republican institutions
in the towns were weakened by bitter party disputes which often
led to civil war. Desire for internal peace led most of the larger
towns to accept the rule of dictators; only Venice remained a
republic, and Venice was dominated by a commercial oligarchy.
Each dictator tried to make his rule hereditary and to build up the
family power until it covered whole provinces. Thus the Sforza
of Milan gained most of Lombardy, while the Medici of Florence
dominated Tuscany. But no dictator ever became strong enough
to annihilate his major rivals; he had to learn how to live with
them. Thus a situation was created not unlike that which existed

in nineteenth-century Europe. There were five great powers—
Venice, Milan, Florence, the Papal States, and the Kingdom of
Naples—and many lesser states. Since no one power was dominant,
each tried to build up a system of alliances to protect its position.
Permanent embassies were established, and the principle of balance
of power was developed. The modern art of diplomacy grew out
of this experience, and was soon imitated by transalpine countries.

Yet, in spite of this skill in diplomacy, one of the great failures
of Renaissance Italy was in the field of politics. Italian states were
too small to have any real political or economic strength. When
France and Spain recovered from their civil wars they easily overran the weak Italian principalities. When the principal trade routes
shifted from the Mediterranean to the Atlantic, the Italians were
too weak to obtain any share of the new commerce. Behind this
obvious material weakness lay a spiritual deficiency. There was
no legitimate government in Italy, no government based on an
ideal which was generally accepted by a majority of the people.
The petty despots of the towns were not anointed kings, so they
could not appeal to the traditional belief in monarchy. No one of
them embodied Italian cultural or political aspirations, so they
could not appeal to the new idea of nationalism. Few men saw any
reason to sacrifice local interests in order to permit a Medici or a
Sforza to dominate north Italy. Thus a united Italy or even a large
kingdom of north Italy was impossible, and the Italians had no
political framework which could channel their superabundant
energy into the work of political and social organization.

The Italians—or at least the dominant urban classes in Italy—
remained Christians, but they had lost confidence in the old ideal
of the leadership of the Church. They had been unable to develop a new political ideal to take the place of the belief they
had lost. Therefore they found it impossible to build a stable
society on the ruins of medieval civilization. They did brilliant

work as individuals, but their contributions became fully effective
only when they were used by the more highly organized societies
of Spain, France, and England.

The fate of Italy is illustrated by the career of Machiavelli
(1469–1527). This man, whose name has become a synonym for
unscrupulous power politics, was actually a convinced republican
and a sincere patriot. He occupied important diplomatic posts
during a brief period when Florence drove out the Medici and re-
established its old republican government. He admired the political
sagacity and civic virtues of the ancient Romans, and hoped that
Florence could preserve its republican institutions by imitating
Roman methods. When the Medici returned to power they were
naturally unwilling to employ a man who had opposed them, and
Machiavelli lost his official positions. Desperately eager to re-
enter politics, Machiavelli wrote the *Prince* in order to call the
attention of the Medici to his skill in political diagnosis. Most of
the book is a completely cold-blooded analysis of the ways in
which the Italian tyrants seized and retained power. Machiavelli
is particularly cynical in his discussion of public opinion: he shows
how a prince may retain a reputation for justice while acting un-
justly and tells his reader that men will forgive the execution of
their fathers more easily than the confiscation of their patri-
monies. But at the end of this amoral treatise on power politics,
Machiavelli added a fervent appeal to Italian nationalism. The
Prince, when he has made himself strong, should unite all Italians
and drive out the foreigners who were already beginning to overrun the peninsula. There is no doubt about his sincerity; this
passage glows with a conviction which is lacking in the earlier
dispassionate analysis. Yet this sincerity only underlines the desperate condition of Italian society. If the only hope for Italy lay
in a Medici despot, if dictatorship were the only road to the proper
organization of Italian society, then the Italian experiment of the
fourteenth and fifteenth centuries had been a failure.

VI. FIRE UNDER THE NORTHERN ASHES

The peoples of the transalpine countries were more attached than the Italians to medieval institutions and ideals. Long after the Italians had struck out confidently along new roads the Northerners were trying stubbornly to preserve their old way of life. Much of this effort seemed to be wasted, but in the long run Northern conservatism was justified. The ideal of legitimate monarchy survived to become the basis for new forms of political organization. The Christian faith survived and gave spiritual justification for the emerging sovereign state. Industrial and commercial techniques, perfected in the last centuries of the Middle Ages, provided a solid material foundation for the civilization of the early modern period.

It is not surprising that the old monarchies became more vigorous toward the end of the Middle Ages. Except in Italy, there was no substitute for traditional kingship. The representative assemblies, which had seemed so strong in the fourteenth century, had never really governed. They had, at times, effectively limited royal power, but they had not gained permanent control of the administrative system. They had been used by the aristocracy to gain political power, but aristocratic influence had meant an endless round of foreign and civil wars. Everyone was tired of disorder and insecurity; even the lesser landholders were weary of being involved in the quarrels of the great lords. As a result, in the fifteenth century, the kings began to receive more support from their people. The revival of monarchical authority began in France at the end of the Hundred Years' War, with the reigns of Charles VII and Louis XI. It came a little later in Spain, when the marriage of Ferdinand and Isabella in 1477 ended a period of civil war. The "new monarchy" in England followed the Wars of the Roses and the advent of the Tudor dynasty in 1485. Even in Germany there was an attempt to revitalize the Empire, and, while this attempt failed, the territorial princes improved their hold over their states.

The remarkable feature of this revival of strong monarchy was the fact that it seldom required the creation of new institutions. The old administrative bureaux, which had held the state together during periods of intrigue and civil war, could now function more effectively. Royal revenue increased and the courts were more successful in repressing disorder. Councils (the heart of the administrative system) which had been dominated by the aristocracy became obedient to the king and were filled with his officials. Representative assemblies continued to meet, but loyally supported royal policy instead of opposing it. It is true that in some countries, notably in France, royal authority was strengthened by the establishment of a standing army, but this was not essential. The Tudors never had a permanent army and yet they came nearer to absolutism than any other English dynasty.

In short, the people of Western Europe had become convinced that the evil of weak government was worse than the evil of strong government and that undeviating loyalty to the king was the only way to prevent disorder and insecurity. Rebellion seemed more dangerous to society than royal tyranny; it was better for individuals to suffer injustice quietly than for them to make protests which might lead to new civil wars. These ideas were extolled by almost all the political theorists of the period and were accepted by the great majority of the people. In actual fact, the "new monarchies" were rather inefficient despotisms, and left a good deal of room for individual initiative within the framework of the security which they had established.

We have already seen that most Europeans remained devoted to the Christian faith in spite of the confusion caused by the troubles of the early fifteenth century. Even in Italy, only a small part of the urban middle class had accepted a completely secular outlook; the great majority of the Italians remained sincere Christians. There were revivalists and reformers in Italy as elsewhere. As late as the 1490's the Renaissance center of Florence surrendered completely, for a brief period, to the puritanical teachings of a Dominican friar, Savonarola. But in Italy the ruling classes, including many of the clergy, had no real interest in religious reform. In the North, on the other hand, kings, nobles, and merchants were all concerned with religious problems. Their interest was often selfish; they wanted to remove the temptation of great wealth from the Church by confiscating some of its property, or to improve the efficiency of ecclesiastical administration by subjecting it to secular control. But they were not always insincere in expressing dismay over the corruption of the Church, and, in order to gain popular support, they often encouraged reformers who were completely honest. Thus a body of opinion was created which demanded reform, even at the price of political interference with the Church.

The popes of this period were completely absorbed in Italian politics and Renaissance culture; they saw neither the danger nor the opportunity which might be afforded by a great religious revival. Since no leadership came from Rome, conscientious clergymen in the North turned increasingly to their kings for support and encouragement. Thus in each country the Church became closely connected with the government. The Protestant Reformation was merely the extreme stage of this process. The kings of France and Spain remained within the Catholic Church largely because they were able to gain special privileges from the pope at the end of the fifteenth century. The rulers of England and north Germany, who had not been so well treated, set up state churches which gave them a large degree of control over the religious life of their countries. But in either case, the clergy became firm supporters of the monarch and taught that secular authorities must be obeyed without question.

In the new alliance between State and Church, the State had the best of the bargain. Its authority was strengthened; primary loyalty was now clearly directed toward secular governments.

On the other hand, the movement toward religious reform was not entirely dependent on state policy, and the widespread religious revival of the sixteenth century could not always be controlled by secular governments. The resulting conflicts between rulers and reformers were not resolved until the seventeenth century. But on the whole, the attempts of the secular states to establish their leadership were reinforced by the moral earnestness of the religious revival. With their ideals once more supporting an effective form of political organization, the transalpine countries began to emerge from the doldrums of the late Middle Ages. Europe was once more ready for a rapid period of growth.

The growth could be rapid because Europe had lost none of its technical skill during the political and spiritual collapse of the fourteenth century. In fact, there had been some notable advances in widely scattered fields during the worst of the disorders. This is a fairly frequent phenomenon, and raises an interesting problem in the history of civilization. If there is steady progress anywhere, it is in the field of technology, and yet this kind of progress seems to have little connection with the stability of society or with the degree to which a civilization satisfies those who participate in it. Just as the introduction of important new techniques in using animal power coincided with the fall of the Roman Empire, so the discovery of new techniques in mining, metallurgy, and measurement of time accompanied the collapse of medieval civilization.

The wars of the late Middle Ages certainly stimulated some of these developments. The introduction of gunpowder early in the fourteenth century is an obvious example. Gunpowder would have had no importance without a group of interrelated experiments and inventions. First of all, metal-workers had to learn how to make cannon which would withstand the force of an explosion. It took some experimenting with alloys and methods of casting to develop a gun which was not as dangerous to the man who touched it off as to the enemy who stood in front of it.

Once this had been accomplished, there was need to improve the trueness of the bore and the roundness of the shot. Then gunsmiths set to work on the problem of building a portable musket. In this way, much was learned about working metal, and all these skills were transferred to other products. At the same time, increased demands for metals stimulated the mining industry. Mines had to be pushed deeper and farther than before; the problem of drainage had to be solved, and thus important engineering techniques were developed.

Other inventions, however, were less directly connected with war. There was no military demand for exact measurement of time, yet the first mechanical clocks were built during this period. Though they were only roughly accurate, they were a great improvement on earlier devices, such as water clocks and marked candles. Medieval craftsmen discovered the basic principle of the escapement mechanism, which in the end would make exact measurement of time possible. Our modern civilization is more time-conscious than any other that has ever existed. If we consider the importance of time measurements in the world today, it is no exaggeration to say that the first mechanical clock was as important in our history as the discovery of America.

There is no need to labor the importance of the invention of printing with movable type. But it should be stressed that the first printing presses were made in the early fifteenth century in medieval Germany, not in Renaissance Italy, and that Italian scholars for a long time scorned the new process. Moreover, the stimulus which led to the invention of printing was the typically medieval desire for cheaper and quicker ways of reproducing religious texts. Without earlier knowledge of the properties of metals the invention would have been impossible, since it was necessary to find an alloy which would expand on cooling and thus give a clear reproduction of the pattern in the type-mould.

There were fewer innovations in navigation and ship-building than in industry during the later Middle Ages. There were some improvements in rigging and in the rudder, but the most important development was the steady acquisition of experience in making long voyages out of sight of land. The Canaries and Madeiras were settled in the fourteenth century, the Azores in the early fifteenth. Men who could find these tiny islands 800 miles out in the Atlantic were already skilled navigators; they had solved almost all the problems which Columbus was to face.

At this point, the "new monarchies" began to influence develop·ments. Most of the kings of the late fifteenth century, unlike their predecessors, were good business men. They appreciated the importance of commerce in adding to the wealth of their countries and hence to their income from taxation. They dreamed of new profits from oceanic navigation. More islands like the Canaries might be found; new fishing grounds might be discovered; perhaps there might even be an all-sea route to the Indies which would break the Italian monopoly on the trade in Eastern luxury goods. Every one of the great voyages of exploration was supported by a Western king. Private individuals could not afford such expeditions, and the Italian cities were not interested in opening up trade-routes which they could not hope to control.

Royal support was grudging and limited, but seldom have small investments produced greater results. The captains of the king of Portugal found the route around Africa to India and the Spice Islands, and made Lisbon the center of a world trading-empire. Spain reluctantly backed Columbus, and gained the mines of Mexico and Peru. England and France, slower to act, were slower to profit, but by the seventeenth century they were rivals for the trade of North America and of India.

It was a long time before the full impact of these discoveries was felt in Europe. Mediterranean trade continued to be important and the Western kings quarreled more bitterly over the possession of Italian towns than over the acquisition of empires in the New World. Even the psychological impact was delayed; few Europeans of the fifteenth or sixteenth centuries realized that they now had a world to exploit instead of a peninsula. But the effects on the economy of Europe were immediate. The great increase in imports of non-European goods, soon followed by an unprecedented influx of precious metals, reinforced an economic revival which had already begun in the second half of the fifteenth century. Economic opportunities increased, and the rigid social and economic patterns imposed by the stagnation of the fourteenth century began to crack. With ideals once more in harmony with institutions, with effective and generally accepted governments, with an expanding economy, Europeans again showed the originality, optimism, and energy which had characterized their first great revival in the twelfth century.

These qualities extended even into the field of art and literature, in which the Italians had been pre-eminent. The late medieval period had not been entirely barren in transalpine Europe, in spite of the prevalence of imitative and derivative work. The tendency toward realism, which we have already seen in Italy, affected the North also, though in the North it was less modified by idealism. Sculptors working on the tombs of kings and nobles created some remarkably lifelike figures; the work of Claus Sluter (d. 1406) at the court of Burgundy is especially fine. At the same time, several important schools of painting developed, in southern France, Germany, and above all, in the Low Countries.

Late medieval sculptors, though technically very skillful, had only a limited range of interests. They appealed primarily to the emotions aroused by scenes of sorrow and death. Their favorite subjects were the sufferings of Jesus, the sorrows of Mary, and the effigies of dead kings and warriors. The painters, on the other hand, were equally skillful technicians, and were interested in a wider range of subjects. They painted religious pictures, portraits, and scenes of daily life. Like the sculptors, they were sometimes so interested in details that they spoiled the effect of the work as a whole. But the greatest Flemish painters, such as Van Eyck and Memling, were worthy rivals of their Italian contemporaries. They were the first to use oil paints and achieved some brilliant color effects with this new medium. They had unusual ability in combining strong religious feeling with realism; their Virgins sit in the upper chamber of comfortable Flemish homes and are adored by prosperous burghers and statesmen.

Late medieval literature had many of the qualities of late medieval art. The great bulk of it was derivative; the old stories were retold in greater detail and the old theme of unrequited love was repeated in more elaborate form. But the best writers were able to combine strong feeling with realism, just as the painters and sculptors had done. The last great medieval allegory, the *Vision of Piers Plowman* by William Langland (d. 1395) is a good example of this quality. Langland, like his predecessors, filled his poem with personifications of virtue and vice, but he also described the society of fourteenth-century England. He was full of moral indignation over the state of both clergy and laity and, though he sympathized with the poorer classes, he was as frank about their gluttony and selfishness as he was about the more elegant vices of the upper classes. Like the other reformers of his time, he sought a religious revival which would bring Church and society back to basic Christian principles.

Chaucer (d. 1400) was a contemporary of Langland, but he took the world as he found it, instead of trying to reform it. He had a comfortable life in government service, and accumulated enough wealth to become a landowner, Justice of the Peace, and member of Parliament. He was interested in human beings, good and bad, wise and foolish, and he understood them better than almost any other medieval writer. His masterpiece was the Prologue to the *Canterbury Tales*, where he described twenty-nine pilgrims about to start the journey to the shrine of St. Thomas. They ranged from the best to the worst of his society, but Chaucer could smile at the little foibles of honorable men just as he could laugh at the roguery of liars and thieves.

Villon (d. 1463) had neither Langland's moral earnestness nor

Chaucer's serene acceptance of human nature. He typified, more than any other writer of the period, the moral and emotional instability of the later Middle Ages. A vagabond at best, and quite possibly a criminal, Villon swung between piety and blasphemy, hope and despair. Like contemporary sculptors, Villon played on the emotions aroused by suffering and fear of death. Within these limits he was a great poet; his feelings seem vivid and real even today.

Many other Northern writers had great technical skill and wide knowledge, though their work seems less interesting today than that of Langland, Chaucer, and Villon. English and German, French and Spanish were well-established literary languages by 1500. The Northern peoples continued their experiments with the drama during this period, and were more advanced in this field than the Italians. Northern scholarship was far from contemptible, especially in science. The first new theories of motion appeared in Oxford and in Paris, and the precursors of Copernicus and Galileo were Northerners rather than Italians. There was even a modest revival of interest in the classics in the North during the late fourteenth and fifteenth centuries.

Thus when the literary and artistic ideas of the Italian Renaissance reached the transalpine countries they had to be adjusted to strong and deep-rooted native traditions. In many ways the rest of Europe treated Italy much as Italy had treated ancient Rome; it borrowed forms and techniques, but infused the new style with its own spirit. Just as a Tudor or a Valois king might learn much from Italian statecraft without taking on all the characteristics of an Italian prince, so a Shakespeare or a Montaigne could be influenced by Italian scholarship without becoming an Italian humanist. In the same way, architects borrowed classical details and decorations from Italy and applied them to buildings which still emphasized Gothic verticality and broken and irregular exterior lines. In the seventeenth century the classical tradition appeared to win a complete victory, but the classicism of the seventeenth century, with its strong tones of Christian discipline, was very different from the classicism of fifteenth-century Italy, with its almost anarchical individualism and undertones of paganism. And behind the classical façade, in the North, lay the older traditions, ready to break out in a Gothic Revival or a Romantic Movement whenever the classical tradition lost its vigor and its novelty.

The sixteenth century was not an easy period for the people of Western Europe. War, rebellion, and religious persecution at times seemed to be destroying the structure of society. But, unlike the fourteenth century, every outbreak of violence was followed by a period of reconstruction. By the end of the century men were working together more effectively than they had for generations; there was greater political security and wider economic opportunity. On these solid foundations a new and larger structure of European civilization could be built.

But the new structure had to be built, for the most part, out of old materials. The modern state, which furnished the central framework for the new civilization, was actually a patchwork of medieval institutions and medieval concepts of law and legitimacy, buttressed by religion. The new economic system, beginning to develop in the direction of capitalism, owed much to Italian bankers and merchants, and even more to the unknown men who had first substituted wind and water power for human muscle, and so had begun to make Europe a land of machinery instead of serfs. The new learning, in its most spectacular achievements, solved problems of medieval science, rather than problems of classical textual criticism.

Thus the modern world preserved, though often in disguise, the essential elements of medieval civilization. It drew strength from these elements, but with medieval achievements it also inherited medieval problems. When should the demands of the state be limited by the rules of law and the interests of religion? When should the free working of the economic system be checked by the needs of society and the principles of Christian brotherhood? How is the conflict between the results of learned investigation and the basic beliefs of religion to be solved? These problems of medieval society have been even greater problems in the modern world. They will continue to be problems as long as our society remembers, in any degree, its medieval origins.

SUGGESTIONS FOR
FURTHER READING

This is a list of books in English which may interest those who wish more detailed information about specific topics in medieval history. Most of these books give further suggestions for reading on the topics with which they deal.

Those who read French will find much that is valuable in the volumes on the Middle Ages in the co-operative *Histoire de France*, edited by Lavisse. Halphen's *Charlemagne et l'empire Carolingien* is also recommended, especially since there is no good treatment of this subject in English. Marc Bloch's two great books—*Les caractères originaux de l'histoire rurale française* and *La société féodale*—have both been translated into English as *French Rural History*, Berkeley, 1966, and *Feudal Society*, Chicago, 1961. R. Fawtier gives some new viewpoints on French history in his book, *Les Capétiens et la France*, available in English as *The Capetian Kings of France* (London, 1960).

No translations of source materials are listed here, since most of them are not very interesting to or easily understood by readers who are acquainted only with the broad outlines of medieval history. There is a useful but unselective list in C. P. Farrer and A. P. Evans, *Bibliography of English Translations from Medieval Sources* (New York, 1946). A selection of the more readable and interesting sources available in English translations is given in the bibliography of *The Middle Ages*, by J. R. Strayer and D. C. Munro.

GENERAL WORKS

BALDWIN, S. *The Organization of Medieval Christianity*. New York, 1929.

BARRACLOUGH, G. *The Origins of Modern Germany*, 2nd ed. Oxford, 1947.

BUTLER, W. F. *The Lombard Communes*. London–New York, 1906.

Cambridge Economic History of Europe. I. *The Agrarian Life of the Middle Ages*. 2nd ed. Edited by M. M. Postan. Cambridge, 1966. II. *Trade and Industry in the Middle Ages*. Edited by M. M. Postan and E. E. Rich. Cambridge, 1952.

Cambridge Medieval History. 8 vols. New York, 1911–1936.

CARLYLE, R. W. and CARLYLE, A. J. *A History of Medieval Political Theory in the West*. 6 vols. Edinburgh-London, 1903–1936.

CRUMP, C. G. and JACOB, E. F. *The Legacy of the Middle Ages*. Oxford, 1932.

DUBY, G. *Rural Economy and Country Life in the Medieval West*. London, 1968.

JOLLIFFE, J. E. A. *The Constitutional History of England to 1485*. 2nd ed. London, 1947.

LEWIS, B. *The Arabs in History*. London, 1950.

LOPEZ, R. S. *The Birth of Europe*. New York, 1967.

McILWAIN, C. H. *The Growth of Political Thought in the West*. New York, 1932.

NEILSON, N. *Medieval Agrarian Economy*. New York, 1936.

OMAN, C. H. *A History of the Art of War. The Middle Ages*. 2 vols. Boston, 1924.

OSTROGORSKY, G. *History of the Byzantine State*. New Brunswick, 1957.

PIRENNE, H. *Economic and Social History of Medieval Europe*. Boston, 1924.

PREVITÉ-ORTON, C. W. *The Shorter Cambridge Medieval History*. 2 vols. Cambridge, 1952.

SALVATORELLI, L. *A Concise History of Italy from Prehistoric Times to Our Own Day*. New York, 1939.

THOMPSON, J. W. *Feudal Germany*. Chicago, 1928.

VASILIEV, A. A. *History of the Byzantine Empire*. 2 vols. Madison, 1928–1929.

CHAPTER I—THE MAKING OF EUROPE

ARRAGON, R. F. *The Transition from the Ancient to the Medieval World*. New York, 1936.

BROWN, P. *The World of Late Antiquity.* New York, 1971.

BURY, J. B. *The Invasion of Europe by the Barbarians.* London, 1928.

COLLINGWOOD, R. G. and MYRES, J. N. L. *Roman Britain and the English Settlements.* Oxford, 1939.

DAWSON, C. *The Making of Europe.* New York, 1934.

DILL, S. *Roman Society in Gaul in the Merovingian Age.* London, 1926.

DOPSCH, A. *The Economic and Social Foundations of European Civilization.* London, 1937. (This is an abridged translation of the 2-vol. German edition, Vienna, 1920–1923.)

GOODENOUGH, E. R. *The Church in the Roman Empire.* New York, 1931.

HODGKIN, R. H. *A History of the Anglo-Saxons.* 2 vols. 2nd ed. Oxford, 1939.

LAISTNER, M. L. W. *Thought and Letters in Western Europe, A.D. 500–900.* New York, 1931.

LOT, F. *The End of the Ancient World and the Beginnings of the Middle Ages.* New York, 1931.

MACMULLEN, R. *Constantine.* New York, 1969.

MOSS, H. St. L. B. *The Birth of the Middle Ages.* Oxford, 1935.

PIRENNE, H. *Mohammed and Charlemagne.* New York, 1939.

RAND, E. K. *Founders of the Middle Ages.* Cambridge (Mass.), 1928.

ROSTOVTZEFF, M. *Social and Economic History of the Roman Empire.* Oxford, 1926.

STENTON, F. M. *Anglo-Saxon England.* 2nd ed. Oxford, 1947.

THOMPSON, E. A. *A History of Attila and the Huns.* Oxford, 1948.

—— *The Early Germans.* Oxford, 1965.

WALLACE-HADRILL, J. M. *The Barbarian West, 400–1000.* London, 1952.

—— *The Long-Haired Kings.* London, 1962.

WHITELOCK, D. *The Beginnings of English Society.* Baltimore, 1963.

WINSTON, R. *Charlemagne: From the Hammer to the Cross.* Indianapolis, 1954.

WOODWARD, E. L. *Christianity and Nationalism in the Later Roman Empire.* London, 1916.

CHAPTER II—THE YEARS OF TRANSITION

BARRACLOUGH, G. *Medieval Germany, 911–1250.* 2 vols. Oxford, 1938.

DVORNIK, F. *The Making of Central and Eastern Europe.* London, 1949.

EVANS, J. *Monastic Life at Cluny.* Oxford, 1931.

GANSHOF, F. L. *Feudalism.* New York, 1952, 1961.

GIBBS, M. *Feudal Order.* New York, 1953.

HASKINS, C. H. *The Normans in European History.* Boston, 1915.

Hitti, P. K. *History of the Arabs*. London, 1953.
Kendrick, T. D. *A History of the Vikings*. New York, 1930.
Kern, F. *Kingship and Law in the Middle Ages*. Oxford, 1939.
Odegaard, C. E. *Vassi and Fideles in the Carolingian Empire*. Cambridge (Mass.), 1945.
Pirenne, H. *Medieval Cities*. Princeton, 1925.
Sawyer, P. H. *The Age of the Vikings*. London, 1962.
Southern, R. W. *The Making of the Middle Ages*. New Haven, 1953.
Stenton, F. M. *The First Century of English Feudalism*. Oxford, 1932.
—— *William the Conqueror*. New York–London, 1908.
Strayer, J. R. *Feudalism*. Princeton, 1965.
Tellenbach, G. *Church, State, and Christian Society at the time of the Investiture Contest*. Oxford, 1940.
Whitney, J. P. *Hildebrandine Essays*. Cambridge, 1932.
Wolfe, P. *The Cultural Awakening*. New York, 1968.

CHAPTER III—THE FLOWERING
OF MEDIEVAL CIVILIZATION

Adams, H. *Mont-Saint Michel and Chartres*. Boston, 1922.
Barraclough, G. *Medieval Germany, 911–1250*. 2 vols. Oxford, 1938.
Brooke, C. *The Twelfth Century Renaissance*. London, 1969.
Conant, K. J. *Early Mediaeval Church Architecture*. Baltimore, 1942.
Haskins, C. H. *The Renaissance of the Twelfth Century*. Cambridge (Mass.), 1927.
—— *The Rise of the Universities*. Cambridge (Mass.), 1923.
Holmes, U. T., Jr. *Daily Living in the Twelfth Century*. Madison (Wisc.), 1952.
Knowles, D. *The Evolution of Medieval Thought*. New York, 1962.
Leff, G. *Medieval Thought*. Harmondsworth, 1958.
Lopez, R. S. *The Commercial Revolution of the Middle Ages*. New York, 1971.
Morey, C. R. *Medieval Art*. New York, 1942.
Munro, D. C. *The Kingdom of the Crusaders*. New York, 1935.
Newhall, R. A. *The Crusades*. New York, 1927.
Painter, S. *French Chivalry*. Baltimore, 1940.
—— *Medieval Society*. Ithaca (New York), 1951.
—— *The Rise of the Feudal Monarchies*. Ithaca (New York), 1951.
Petit-Dutaillis, C. *The Feudal Monarchy in France and England from the Tenth to the Thirteenth Century*. London, 1936.
Plucknett, T. F. T. *A Concise History of the Common Law*, 4th ed. London, 1948.

POLLOCK, F. and MAITLAND, F. W. *The History of English Law before the Time of Edward V.* 2 vols. 2nd ed. Cambridge, 1899.

RASHDALL, H. *Universities of Europe in the Middle Ages.* 3 vols. Rev. ed. Oxford, 1936.

RUNCIMAN, S. *A History of the Crusades.* Cambridge, 1951–1954.

SETTON, K. M., ed. *A History of the Crusades.* 2 vols. Madison, 1969.

STENTON, D. M. *English Society in the Early Middle Ages (1066–1307).* 3rd ed. Baltimore, 1962.

WADDELL, H. *The Wandering Scholars.* Boston–New York, 1927.

CHAPTER IV—THE MEDIEVAL SUMMER

Many of the books listed for Chapter III (12th century) also cover the period of this chapter (13th century).

COULTON, G. G. *Five Centuries of Religion.* Cambridge, 1927.

FRANKL, P. *Gothic Architecture.* Harmondsworth, 1962.

GILSON, E. *The Spirit of Medieval Philosophy.* 1930.

KANTOROWITZ, E. *Frederick the Second.* London, 1931.

LEA, H. C. *A History of the Inquisition of the Middle Ages.* 3 vols. New York, 1887.

LUCHAIRE, A. *Social France in the Age of Philip Augustus.* New York, 1912.

McKECHNIE, W. S. *Magna Carta.* 2nd ed. Glasgow, 1914.

PACKARD, S. R. *Europe and the Church under Innocent III.* New York, 1927.

PAINTER, S. *The Reign of King John.* Baltimore, 1949.

—— *William Marshall.* Baltimore, 1933.

POWICKE, F. M. *King Henry III and the Lord Edward.* 2 vols. Oxford, 1947.

—— *The Thirteenth Century (1216–1307).* Oxford, 1953. (Deals only with England.)

PREVITÉ-ORTON, C. W. *A History of Europe from 1198 to 1378.* New York, 1937.

SABATIER, P. *Life of St. Francis of Assisi.* New York, 1894.

SAPORI, A. *The Italian Merchant in the Middle Ages.* New York, 1970.

SEDGWICK, H. D. *Italy in the Thirteenth Century.* New York, 1928.

STRAYER, J. R. *The Albigensian Crusades.* New York, 1971.

CHAPTER V—THE LONG AUTUMN

BOASE, T. S. R. *Boniface VIII.* London, 1933.

BURCKHARDT, J. *The Civilization of the Renaissance in Italy.* (There are many editions, e.g., Modern Library, 1954.)
CARTELLIERI, A. *The Court of Burgundy.* New York, 1929.
CHAMPION, P. *Louis XI.* New York, 1929.
EHRENBERG, R. *Capital and Finance in the Age of the Renaissance.* New York, 1928.
FERGUSON, W. *The Renaissance.* New York, 1940.
GRAY, H. L. *The Influence of the Commons on Early Legislation.* Oxford, 1932.
HAY, D. *Europe in the Fourteenth and Fifteenth Centuries.* New York, 1966.
HUIZINGA, J. *The Waning of the Middle Ages.* London, 1924.
JACOB, E. F. *Essays in the Conciliar Epoch.* Manchester, 1943.
KRISTELLER, P. O. *Renaissance Thought.* 2 vols. New York, 1961, 1965.
───── *Renaissance Philosophy and the Medieval Tradition.* Latrobe, 1966.
LAPSLEY, G. T. *Crown, Community, and Parliament in the Later Middle Ages.* Oxford, 1951.
MERRIMAN, R. *Rise of the Spanish Empire.* Vol. I. New York, 1918.
MISKIMIN, H. A. *The Economy of Early Renaissance Europe 1300–1460.* Englewood Cliffs, 1969.
MOWAT, R. B. *Wars of the Roses.* London, 1914.
MYERS, A. R. *England in the late Middle Ages.* Harmondsworth, Middlesex, 1952.
ORIGO, I. *The Merchant of Prato.* New York, 1957.
PERROY, E. *The Hundred Years War.* New York, 1951.
POWER, E. and POSTAN, M. M. *Studies in English Trade in the Fifteenth Century.* London, 1933.
PREVITÉ-ORTON, C. W. *A History of Europe from 1198 to 1378.* New York, 1937.
STEEL, A. *Richard II.* Cambridge, 1941.
THOMPSON, J. W. *Economic and Social History of Europe in the Later Middle Ages.* New York, 1931.
TREVELYAN, G. M. *England in the Age of Wycliff.* Various eds. London, 1899.

INDEX